THE ROAD TO [illegible]

The Diary of Basil Walker-Taylor Dec 1941 to Feb 1942

Edited by Paddy Walker-Taylor

Walker-Taylor

Published by Walker-Taylor

Printed and Bound in Great Britain by
The Good News Press Ltd
Hallsford Bridge, Ongar
Essex CM5 9RX

ISBN 978-0-9561930-0-1

CONTENTS

INTRODUCTION

The Road to Singapore is the diary of my father, Basil Walker-Taylor, during the three months before the fall of Singapore to the Japanese in February 1942.

He was 40, working as a surveyor for Government, and living near Alor Star in Northern Malaya with his wife Pat when the first Japanese planes were sighted. They packed their possessions and headed south, but they soon had to part. He enlisted in the Federated Malay States Volunteer Force and had many interesting experiences, but after a few weeks was relieved to be able to transfer an Indian Artillery regiment where he knew one or two of the officers and felt he could be more useful doing survey work, as he knew the territory. They moved slowly south towards Singapore, mostly under fire. He was able to visit Pat from time to time in Singapore and eventually ensured her departure on one of the last passenger boats ('The Gorgon'). He himself tried to find a boat to escape, but in vain, and he eventually re-joined his regiment which surrendered to the Japanese. The diary ends at this point, but he was interned in Changi Gaol in Singapore for the duration. It is likely that he wrote the diary from memory whilst in Changi, taking care to conceal its existence from his captors.

On release from Changi, he was reunited with Pat in Australia in September 1945, and they resumed life in Malaya. They had two children, Paddy and Cecilia. His final posting was as Chief Surveyor, Singapore. He retired in 1959 and they moved first to Ireland, and then to Pangbourne in England, where he died in August 1983.

Paddy Walker-Taylor
Rickmansworth January 2009

CHAPTER 1

Alor Star to Ipoh

7th December 1941

I was woken out of a deep sleep at 4.15am by the shrilling of a railway engine. My wife, Pat, was alongside me, still sleeping peacefully. I imagined that war might have broken out and this train was rushing reinforcements or arms to the frontier. Then I told myself I was being foolish because we would have been warned by telephone if it had been war - and I fell asleep again.

I rose at about 6.30 am as usual, and sat down for a while at my desk in the room next to the bedroom. The boy brought in a cup of tea and some fruit on a tray and placed them on a small table alongside.

Then I heard the sound of several explosions in the distance. From our front sitting room, I could see one of the hangers of the Alor Star aerodrome, about five miles away. A number of planes were circling and there were puffs of smoke in the sky. Pat joined me at the window. It was clear to us that Japanese planes, probably from aircraft carriers, had been on a bombing mission. A short time later, Blenheim bomber after Blenheim bomber zoomed up and sped eastwards.

We listened to the Singapore news broadcast at 7.30 am - Pearl Harbour had been attacked by aircraft - Hong Kong and Singapore likewise - and a landing had been made by the enemy in small numbers in Kelantan, on the east coast.

I thought our house was unlikely to be in any immediate danger, as it was two miles from Alor Star town and five miles from the aerodrome. However, I suggested to Pat that if any enemy aircraft did fly overhead while I was at work, she should shelter in the ditch bordering our drive.

We ate a hasty breakfast, and I got to my office an hour earlier than usual, about 8.15 am. My job was Assistant Food Controller for the State of Kedah. My boss, Mather, arrived soon afterwards. We agreed to put into action certain schemes which had been drawn up in the event of war, although we knew they were far from perfect. The truth was, that although we had had long discussions beforehand about what was to be done, at heart, we had never really thought of war as being close to our homes. We had not really pictured enemy aeroplanes flying overhead all day - which they were doing now in flights of thirty or more. Nor had we honestly considered the likelihood of bombs being dropped at any moment right in our midst.

The main issues were how to feed the 40,000 townsfolk if food stocks were burned, and how to guard stocks from rioters and thieves.

To a large extent, Kedah was the granary for the rest of Malaya. All rice millers in the state would have to be threatened or bullied into keeping their businesses going. All old stocks of padi must be milled as the new crop of rice was almost ready for harvesting. It was imperative too that food shops were kept open.

Our problem was that many shopkeepers just wanted to shut their shops and get away from the town. This was hardly surprising since ARP wardens had warned them on many earlier occasions of the dangers of falling masonry and fires which could be started by incendiary bombs. The Police had also staged realistic rehearsals of how riots and street fights would be quelled.

I left the office and visited a couple of rice mills, telling the millers that they were being relied on to carry on as usual and that any attempt at profiteering would be severely dealt with. They promised their full co-operation.

I eventually got back home at 6 o'clock, very tired. Pat and I had tea and went for a walk to the Club. It was sprinkling with rain. There was no one at the Club, not even a boy in sight - they had probably all bolted!

We listened to the news. Singapore had been raided twice, but the Japs had been repelled in Kelantan. Sungei Patani (150 miles to the South of us) had been bombed, and a hit scored on the aerodrome, destroying a petrol dump.

8th December

Japanese planes flew overhead all day. A few Bofors guns near the town fired at them intermittently, but their shooting was poor.

Pat worked hard packing, helped by cookie, syce, kebun, amah and a Chinese packer from town. Poor Pat had a difficult day as the aerodrome was bombed consistently. The Ack Ack guns did their best to drive them off. Air-raid alarms sounded every half-hour and Pat had to run outside each time and lie in the ditch. She said that on one occasion she had had the shock of her life when a terrific report went off suddenly just behind her. At first, she thought it was a bomb, and then realised it was one of our anti-aircraft guns firing.

A large bomber crashed in the rice fields about a mile away. We heard later that it was an RAF Blenheim piloted by Pongo Scarfe. He had been bombing Singgora and received wounds in the chest from machine gun bullets. He was so weak by the time he got back to Alor Star that he couldn't steer his plane properly, and it crashed. He was alive when taken out of the plane, but died later in hospital*.

Pat wanted to stay in Alor Star, so we put it to the British Adviser (the 'B.A.'), J.D.Hall. He agreed there was no urgent danger, so Pat could stay on. She and Mrs Mather would be the only two women remaining, apart from some of the hospital sisters. He invited Pat and I to stay at the Residency, and we went around at about 7 pm that evening. Actually, I think the B.A. was as pleased to have us with him as we were to accept his hospitality. The peace and quiet luxury of the Residency was very gratifying after the rush and disorder of our own quarters, but the Residency was about a quarter of a mile from the main road and all night we could hear a constant stream of traffic going to the front.

9th December

On my way to the office, I was pleased to see hundreds of Gurkhas marching along the road. They looked efficient, purposeful and tough.

Pat went back to our quarters after breakfast to finish packing as she still had quite a lot to do. My day was just a wild rush: giving instructions to subordinates and seeing that they were carried out; dealing with complaints by rice

* Pongo Scarfe was awarded a posthumous VC after the war

dealers that certain millers would not supply them with rice; and other complaints that both dealers and millers were over-charging, etc, etc. There was also a continuous stream of complaints about food dealers and coffee shops putting up their shutters. All of this called for swift and effective action. Supply officers in other districts kept ringing to get advice over similar problems.

It was reported that the largest miller in Sungei Patani district had absconded and his mill had stopped milling. I paid a quick visit to the mill to find that most of the coolies had run away. The Japs had bombed the mill the previous day and had killed and wounded a number of coolies, although doing very little damage to the mill itself or the rice stocks. However, visits to several other mills showed that they all had their reserve stocks intact and milling was carrying on apace.

Back in Alor Star, I found most of the food shops had shut and I spent an hour forcing them to open up again. Some owners, however, had fled. The streets were practically deserted, but this always occurred after an air-raid warning. After a while, people would appear again in the streets, and one or two daring coffee shop keepers would open their front doors an inch or two.

Back in the office, there were dozens of matters needing attention. Mather asked if I would go to Sungei Patani the next day and take charge of Food Control in the southern and central parts of the state.

The sound of gunfire seemed enormously close. However, the BA, who had been in conferences with the Divisional Commander (General Murray Lyon), told me that the General was very optimistic and had said that a counter-attack had been successful. The General came to dinner at the Residency that night and appeared to be quite unmoved or put out at all. Kemp and Armstrong were also staying at the Residency, acting as aides-de-camp to the B.A. Kemp was in charge of the air-aid warning organisation, but it was already showing signs of cracking badly.

The B.A. agreed with me that it was time for Pat to evacuate. I could drive her down myself to Kulim and then back north to Sungei Patani. She was very disappointed.

She had finished packing our things during the day. However, despite all our efforts, there was now no chance of getting any of our belongings away by train, as all space from Alor Star was reserved for the military.

10th December

I sent the syce and amah off in the little Morris with most of Pat's personal luggage to Kulim. Pat and I followed in the Chrysler with a couple more cabin trunks. On the way, we called in at several mills, and we eventually got to Kulim about midday. There, I saw Graham, who was in charge of things generally. He arranged for Pat to stay with the Public Works Department people, and asked if I would take Mrs Scarfe back with me to Alor Star. After her husband's death she had evacuated to Kulim with the rest of the Air Force wives, but had then decided she would carry on with her job nursing at the Alor Star Civil hospital.

It was horrid having to say goodbye to Pat, but she was very brave and didn't break down. I felt wretched.

I picked up Mrs Scarfe, and we got to Sungei Patani about 3 pm. I heard that Penang had been heavily raided earlier in the day and was in chaos. Ipoh also.

I had food control work to do in Sungei Patani, including a visit to Rear Divisional Headquarters, where Shears told me they were all in a flap about a report that parachutists had descended ten miles to the north.

When I eventually set off back again to Alor Star, the journey was uneventful, apart from several stops on the road caused by Jap planes overhead.

Kemp had invited back to dinner a couple of AA gunner officers who had billeted themselves on the verandah of the Supreme Court. They seemed nice youths, but very young and callow. They had only been in the country a week or two, having come out by troop ship with a draft of young gunner officers. They told me that the way they had been selected for the various batteries was the same way that slaves were purchased! They themselves had been assigned to the Hong Kong/ Singapore Royal Artillery - manned entirely by Indians - although these lads couldn't speak a word of Hindustani!

11th December

Arriving at the office the following morning, I found a memo to the effect that salaries and wages for the month should be paid that day. I asked my deputy, Ahmat, to get on with this work and buried myself in Food Control duties.

There were many air-raid warnings and Bofors guns stationed all around the Government Offices (of all places!) blazed away with no effect.

After lunch, I found that the salary schedules were in a terrific muddle and Ahmat had lost his nerve, turning sullen and bad-tempered. It was impossible to reason with him or get any sense out of him. Whilst talking to him, I was asked to go to the B.A.'s office, where I received the code words "Curtain Down". That was the signal for swift evacuation. It was a terrific surprise to me because I had no inkling that the end was so near.

Kemp and Armstrong and the two clerks rushed around with armfuls of papers to be burnt. Howett remained calm and seemed to be directing affairs capably. I went back to the Survey Office and paid the staff and the coolies who were around. I saw to it that all of the large-scale maps, and the few confidential papers, were destroyed.

My car was parked outside the Government buildings, and surprisingly my syce was still there. I thought he would have cleared off as soon as he heard of the evacuation. I told him that I could take him and his wife and child to Sungei Patani, but he preferred not to go with me. So I paid him his wages up to the month-end, bade him farewell, and drove back to the Residency.

Ah Seow, the cook, was capable and efficient. Together, we strapped my cabin trunk and some suitcases on the back of the car and crammed in as many of our belongings and Ah Seow's as we could into the dicky-seat and the car interior. I released the poor old parrot from his cage. I reassured the rest of the Residency servants that the B.A. would make arrangements for their transport to Kulim and would be there in person shortly. We left for Sungei Patani. The car was in first rate condition and went like a bird.

The road was crowded with refugees - cars and lorries packed to overflowing with masses of humanity and their belongings. Whole families on foot carrying as much as they could - toddlers firmly clutching a bucket or a couple of hens - Chinese drawing pigs in front of them - Indians leading recalcitrant goats. Cyclists, motors, pedestrians, hand-cart pushers, men, women and children all thronged together.

The Malays were conspicuous by their absence from the roads - although the roadside coffee-shops seemed to have more than their usual complement of Malay idlers - squatting and standing around. Padi planters carried on with their work calmly and slowly, with hardly a glance to spare for the heavy traffic that sped by.

I gave some papers and maps which I had picked up on leaving the Government buildings to Ah Seow to tear in small pieces as we proceeded on our way.

I stopped at two rice mills and warned the millers that we were evacuating Alor Star and that it would only be a day or two before they would over-run by the enemy.

The road was quite dangerous, because military transport of all kind was driving around furiously. On occasions we had to pull into the side of the road to wait until a convoy passed. We eventually got to Sungei Patani about five o'clock, and I went to Biddulph's house. He asked me to stay with him as he had sent his wife and children off to Australia the day before. Then Bancroft arrived, with about a dozen strangers who turned out to be newspaper correspondents of all nationalities (including The New York Times, Sydney Sun, and Sydney Herald). Drinks were brought, and these people showed no sign of going until they had finished all of Biddulph's whisky. I thought they might have pushed off earlier, as they had nothing to talk about and were merely eager for information.

After a while I went around to O'Connell's house. O'Connell was in charge of transport and I wanted to arrange for lorries to carry rice to Kulim and Bandur Bharu. He told me that he had just completed arrangements to transport 5,000 estate labourers to Gurun the next morning to work on switchworks for a new position. The Military authorities had asked estate managers to co-operate in the scheme, and at last all was ready. A hundred lorries were to take fifty coolies per lorry from Sungei Patani at 5.30 am the following morning.

I was very interested in this scheme and asked if I could have the hundred lorries between the time they arrived at Gurun and the time that they were needed in the evening to bring the coolies back. My idea was to load up each lorry with rice from some of the mills nearby and return to Gurun. I estimated that, with luck, two or maybe three trips per lorry should be possible. O'Connell agreed, and I returned to Biddulph's place. The B.A. and his staff (Howitt, Kemp, and Armstrong) also arrived at about the same time. Bancroft and some other people were also present.

I moved quarters to Bancroft's house after having told the B.A. of my plans for the following day. We went on to the Club which was fairly full of elderly planters and a few officers and war correspondents and a few A.R.P. officials off-duty. Drinks were poured and lowered quite rapidly.

When we finally returned to Bancroft's house, O'Connell rang to say that the B.A. had agreed that the convoy could move off at 5.30 am. However, at about 4.00 am the B.A. rang again and told us to move to Kulim immediately, as the enemy appeared to have broken through our defences. Fighting was apparently already occurring on Harvard Estate, about ten miles north of Sungei Patani. We packed hurriedly, and inside an hour were on our way.

12th December

The journey from Sungei Patani was uneventful, until we were about a mile outside Kulim, when I saw a large charabanc flashing past in the opposite direction. It was full of European women - and among them was Pat! Recognition was mutual but we could do nothing but wave to each other. It seemed that she was being evacuated to Ipoh or Taiping, and this was confirmed a few minutes later by Graham at the Police Station in the centre of the town. The scene at the Police Station was extraordinary. Thousands of natives were milling around. A few Europeans were there too, but none of them knew what to do as they had received no orders other than to proceed to Kulim. No one knew the military situation.

I walked around the town to see whether food was being sold at the proper prices. Lots of the shops had shut. Most of us then went on to the Club and ate a hearty breakfast. Then, the B.A. arrived. My orders were to carry on with food control duties, implementing any measures I thought necessary. So Bancroft and I returned, calling at Freddie Meyrick's en route. His place was full of planters - mostly in Special Police uniform, and all very annoyed that the Gurun scheme had been disrupted. It seemed that the order to evacuate Sungei Patani was due to misinformation given to the B.A. by Boissier. The planters had worked hard getting coolies to volunteer for the job - and had provided spades, arranged supervision and so on. They felt that bungling at the head of affairs was hard to excuse, and that if more coolies were required for a similar job in the future, it would be difficult to recruit them.

Returning to Sungei Patani, it was like a city of the dead. Bancroft and Biddulph had somehow managed to get the ARP and other emergency services functioning again, and Blackman concentrated on impressing all available motor vehicles. In fact, transport arrangements had not functioned well ever since hostilities commenced. Any lorry left unattended was liable to be picked up by the Military or anyone who required a lorry. The other trouble was drivers. The only way to be certain of keeping a driver was to keep him in sight all the time, and of course that was impossible.

Blackman agreed that I could take a dozen lorries to bring rice from Gurun to Kulim. There were dozens of lorries at the Transport Officer's park but most of them were defective or missing ignition keys (although the latter was a problem that could be overcome fairly easily).

The hospital had asked for food, mainly rice, but they also wanted eggs, beef, mutton. Commodities like this were out of the question, but we managed to break into several shops and, to the best of our ability, gave the hospital what it required. Armstrong assisted me in all this and he worked uncommonly well. Nothing was too much trouble to him.

Armstrong and I then got hold of ten lorries and drivers. After filling up with petrol, we drove to a village, Sungei Lalang, about ten miles north of Sungei Patani where I had heard that a Chinese estate supplier held large food stocks. We also called in on the large rice dealers and took a large part of their rice stocks and most of their flour, sugar, salt, and milk. I gave them all receipts on the Kedah Government.

On filling each lorry with rice, it was sent to wait near the main road. Once loading was complete, I headed for the first lorry and Armstrong for the last to start the return journey. However, when I got there, the driver was missing. We shouted, tooted the horn, and looked for him, but after ten minutes I decided that he had got the breeze up (we were near the front with the sound of occasional gunfire). The ignition key was missing and I was about to disconnect the ignition wires to start the lorry, when the driver suddenly appeared, very frightened indeed. It seemed that some Punjabi troops had found him sitting in his lorry. They were unable to speak Malay, or he to speak Urdu, and they took him for a Fifth Columnist. They pulled him along to an officer who gave orders that he be shot forthwith - but he was saved by the timely appearance of another officer who spoke a little Malay!

We returned to Sungei Patani with the loot and phoned Mather, who had set up his headquarters in Kulim, to tell him that the convoy would reach him shortly. Two constables took our places in the lorries.

Armstrong and I managed to collect another dozen lorries, and we set out once again for Gurun. I took a constable with me this time as I anticipated trouble getting the Chinese coolies to load the rice if the miller was absent. Indeed, on arrival at the mill, the coolies were most unhelpful. It was only when I took the rifle from the constable and threatened the Chinese person who I took to be the mandor that they agreed to get on with the job of loading - which was then done most expeditiously!

We took fifty out of fifteen hundred tons of rice in the mill. In the process, a Malay who said he was Tungku [*ie prince*] someone or other, and a relation of the Kedah Royal House, approached me and said that the Sultan had an estate adjoining the mill and that the employees there had no food, so would I please do something. After satisfying myself that his story was true, I let him have ten bags. I gave the Chinese a chit on the Kedah Government for the Government rice and one on the Sultan for the Malay's rice.

We sent the convoy off to Kulim as before, and managed to collect another five lorries for yet another trip to the mill. By this time, it was almost dark, and when we got to the mill all the coolies had fled. A visit to several rice dealers in Gurun also proved abortive, so we had no alternative but to return to Sungei Patani.

Back in Sungei Patani it was raining. Drivers of cars and lorries complained that none of the coffee shops would open up for trade, so attempts had to be made to get them to open up, and a few did.

I found my headlights had fused. I tried the old trick with tin foil, but the resultant light would only last for a few seconds before fusing again. How I missed my syce! However, a lorry driver came to my assistance, and after a while got my lights going. I drove to ARP headquarters where Bancroft and a number of native wardens were on duty - mainly playing cards or doing crosswords. I found a vacant chair and fell asleep in a couple of ticks, to be awakened at midnight by Ken Bancroft with an invitation to go to someone's place for dinner. I can't recollect his name, but he lived in the first floor above two shops in Sungei Patani.

Sungei Patani had not received any direct hits, but the aerodrome, on the outskirts of the town, had received attention from bombers all day. At Bancroft's house, bombs had exploded 100 yards away. So far, no night bombing. As it transpired, the Japs did not indulge in night bombing during the whole Malayan hostilities. However, the fear of it was ever-present, and we all took full precautions.

None of the few Europeans in Sungei Patani knew anything of the military situation, and nor did any of the officers whom we met passing through. All they seemed to know was that the enemy were South of Alor Star, and that the two bridges had been blown. Earlier in the day, I had met John Scott (a Battery commander of the 22nd Mountain Regiment), who told me that he had lost all his guns somewhere around Jitra owing to a surprise advance of the enemy, and he was going to Penang to get some more. He did not appear to be unduly worried.

<u>13th December</u>

Cookie and Bancroft's boy had managed to get hold of sufficient food from somewhere to provide a decent breakfast. Armstrong and I then got on with the job of trying to find transport. It wasn't easy, because lorries were needed to evacuate families for Emergency Services (hospital patients, staff etc) and Army Transport Officers were removing any lorries they found in the streets - despite the protests of the drivers who slept in them!

After a while, I left Armstrong to it, and went to the market in the town which I tried to get up and running. It was in a stinking condition - inches deep in rotting fruit and vegetables, and all the gutters were blocked and full of fetid water. I had to threaten immediate imprisonment just to persuade a number of the stall-holders to do some cleaning up. I went to all the food dealers and forced them to open their doors - but none kept them open for longer than it took me to get fifty yards up the road. Police were scarce, and my orders were difficult to enforce.

At about four in the afternoon, we were told to evacuate Sungei Patani. Graham offered me accommodation in his quarters in Kulim, although he already had Bancroft, J.D.Hall, Kemp, Howett, Armstrong, and several others staying there. Most of us slept on the floor in the sitting room. The military situation was still obscure, and I don't think that even the B.A. knew what was happening.

14th December

Still no further news, although we had the impression that our flight might have to continue. I went to the Club with some others for breakfast. It was well located, being alongside the District Office. Mather was in an office nearby and he seemed to be quite happy with the food supplies that I had sent down in the past few days. I contented myself with checking that most food shops were functioning and that the market was running more or less properly.

Kulim had not been bombed, being off the main Penang-Siam road, and local people were not really aware that war was close by. However, during the day a large number of Chinese and Indians suddenly decided that it would be safer further South. At least one of our Food Control lorries disappeared as a result of sudden panic by the driver. Bancroft let his driver return to Sungei Patani to collect his wife and children. I told him he would be lucky to see his car again.

I rang Pat during the day. She was staying with her sister and brother-in-law, Elsie and Bill Hall (who was a Chief

Police officer), and I got through to her surprisingly easily. She was in good spirits, and I told her I would probably be coming through shortly. It was a thrill to hear her voice again for we had never been apart for more than twenty hours in all our married life*.

On the radio, there was no mention of Kedah or any withdrawal. Comments about the war in Malaya were confined to Kelantan and Kuantan. I heard of one Jap plane that had flown low over Kulim the day before, pursuing an RAF plane. The Malay Asistant Superintendant of Police had ordered police in the compound to aim their rifles at the plane which flew over at a height of only 80 feet. He did not give the order to fire, thinking of the likely loss of civilian life if the plane had crashed in Kulim.

Graham once again entertained the large party to tiffin and dinner, and again I slept on the sitting-room floor. The poor B.A. was up most of the night making and receiving calls to military HQ. Some of these were important but some were trifling. I pitied the poor man because he could not have had much sleep since hostilities commenced. Most of the calls were from the telegraph office in code and had to be checked carefully, as a mistaken letter might make all the difference.

15th December

The B.A. got word during the night that the game was up in Kedah, and he warned us all to prepare to move. I went around to the Engineer's house where Pat had been staying, and picked up most of her suitcases. I took care to include

* They had married on 23rd April 1938, almost four years earlier

her cabin trunk as I thought she had told me the previous day that her valuable stamp collection was in it. Luggage space was rather limited, because, in addition to Cookie and a few of his belongings, I had to bring Bancroft and his suitcases, as his car had indeed failed to return from Sungei Patani.

After breakfast, we went to the Survey Office and loaded up a lorry with all the instruments, stationery and standard sheet tracings that we thought might be of military use, to go to the Survey Office, Kuala Lumpur. We destroyed all maps and confidential papers that we thought might be of value to the enemy and set off for Taiping to report for duty to the British Resident, Perak. On the way, we passed several demolition parties on the way preparing to demolish bridges, and reached Taiping about two in the afternoon.

Whilst I was in sitting in the car in front of the Resident's office, I saw a bus draw up and in it, to my astonishment, I saw Ah Qwee – who was the cook's wife, who also acted as Pat's amah. She was weeping copiously and clutching her adopted child to her breast. Ah Seow, her husband, who was in the car with me, saw her at the same time as I did, and leapt out of the dicky seat and rushed over to the bus and began to berate her furiously at the top of his voice in Chinese. I noticed that some of J.D.Hall's servants were also in the bus.

It appears that after arriving in Kulim, Ah Qwee had begun to lose her nerve and to long for the reassuring presence of Ah Seow. Pat had reasoned with her and managed to calm her down, but when Kulim was evacuated and they both went on to Ipoh, she became worse than ever and would not be comforted. She became obsessed with the idea that Ah Seow would not know where she was, and that it was her duty to return to Kulim and begin the search for him there. Despite Pat's offer to send her to Singapore where she had friends, she would not be diverted. She had met some of the other Kedah Residency servants in Ipoh who for some reason were being returned to Taiping, and it was there that we so fortuitously encountered her. Ah Seow wouldn't listen to any of her protests of being worried on his behalf and he gave her a thorough scolding. I gather he ended by saying that as she had so stupidly left Pat's guardianship, she could stew in her own juice and remain in Taiping whilst he carried on to Ipoh with me. I was sorry for her, but it certainly served her right, for, apart from her stupidity, her lack of gratitude in deserting Pat at such a critical time deserved no sympathy.

When I finally got to the Resident's office, the B.A. was already there, and he told Bancroft and me that we had better go to Ipoh. He suggested that the FMSVF [*Federated Malay States Volunteer Force*] might be glad of us. This was precisely what Bancroft and I wanted, so we headed to Ipoh, stopping for a few minutes at Kuala Kangsar whilst I rang Pat to forewarn her of my arrival.

What a joy it was to be with Pat once more! We were both transported! The only disappointment to both of us was that I had apparently misunderstood her on the telephone earlier regarding the stamps. In reality, they were not in the cabin trunk I had brought with me, but in a suitcase which I had left behind in Kulim.

We arranged for Bancroft to stay with Pat's brother, Derek, and his wife, Olive. The relaxation after the strain of the past was most enjoyable and it was pleasant to be with one's own people. However, I was sorry for Elsie, because she had been to such trouble getting her children, Cedric and Robert, over to Malaya for Christmas, and now she was at her wits end about the future as far as they were concerned. She had sent them to Mrs Barr [*Pat's mother*] in Singapore where they would be safe for the time being. Pat and Elsie had been working in the Auxiliary Medical Service each day, helping to look after civilians wounded by machine gun bullets and bomb splinters during air-raids. I think there had been several air-raids that day.

Later on, after dinner, we went around to Derek's house for drinks. Olive was there but Derek was in Kuantan.

That night, Pat and I agreed that I should report to the FMSVF the following day. The important thing was to do one's best for the war effort. It seemed things were very critical just now. We would make a stand shortly and drive the Japs back. After that, I would think about promotion for myself.

<u>16th December</u>

Shortly after breakfast, we heard an air-raid alarm followed by the sound of bombs. As many as 15 Jap planes flew over our house, presumably en route back to their base at Singgora.

The next excitement was the arrival of an elderly European who brought around the latest order from the Resident which was for all European women in Ipoh to evacuate as far south as possible with the least possible delay. Preferably not to Singapore, as Singapore was already becoming overcrowded with refugees. This was a colossal surprise for we all felt that we would be safe in Ipoh for at least another week. Elsie immediately decided to pack the household effects and send them on to Singapore. She did this forthwith, with Pat's assistance.

Bill decided to set up an office administering the Police Department at home, attending his main office only when strictly necessary. He felt that his house was a much less of a bomb target than the Chief Officer's office, and because he was always required to set an example to his staff by taking cover every time an ARP warning sounded, he would waste far less time. He had been up most of the night on the telephone (as he had on previous nights) and it was obvious he would be unable to carry on efficiently unless he tried to rest whenever the opportunity arose - night or day. A downstairs room was earmarked for the office.

I went in to Ipoh to buy razor blades etc. The town was in quite a mess. Lots of shops had been bombed and shattered, others were gutted by fire, and several bomb craters gaped in the road. It was fortunate that the Japs had not dropped any of their large bombs, as otherwise the loss of life would have been many times larger. I saw David Beattie standing on the pavement outside a Medical Centre and he appeared to be in jovial spirits. I got the razor blades from Cold Storage, and Bancroft and I also purchased about $50 worth of tinned food there to present to Bill. People were dropping in on him all day and his liabilities as a host must have been large. Tinned food was going to be difficult to obtain shortly.

Lunch at Bill's was a very scratch affair with many people present. Afterwards, I made my will (which Bill witnessed) leaving everything to Pat. I handed it over to her with bank-books, scrip etc. Packing was not difficult as I took only a small suitcase and a kit bag filled with toilet necessaries - shorts, shirts, dozens of handkerchiefs, sarongs and bajus, shoes and socks, towels, pillow and mosquito net. I also took my large photograph of Pat, taken by Dorothy Wading when on leave. I handed my car over to Bill who agreed to impress it for police purposes.

At about 4 o'clock, after a sad parting from my sweet little wife, Bancroft and I went to the FMSVF headquarters at the Turf Club, and presented ourselves for enlistment.

CHAPTER 2

Enlistment in FMSVR

16th December 1941 (ctd)

Despite the fact I was already a member of the KVF, it was decided that I should enlist afresh, and I was accordingly posted to a hybrid section of a company called A/Support Battery. I was disappointed that Bancroft had been posted elsewhere - as a clerk at FMSVF Brigade headquarters.

That afternoon I was issued with most of the essential equipment, except boots, as there were none of my size, and a pack. No beds were issued, but I found some planks and constructed a makeshift bed in a horse stall. No one took the trouble to explain any of my duties to me, or to help me to familiarise myself with my surroundings. Apparently the Turf Club was a recruits' dumping ground!

It was quite clear that the Volunteer organisation was not a smooth one. Had it not been for the individual initiative of certain of the men it is difficult to imagine how they would have carried on. Certainly the officers were ignorant of their first duty, which was to look after the well-being of their men.

At 6 o'clock, I was told I would have to go on guard duty at 7.30, and after a poor meal of insufficient and badly cooked food, another man and I took up duty at the main gate. We alternated two hours on duty and two off. Apparently men could be ill-spared for guards. The Guard Commander was a Malay guard - a pleasant enough oaf who was a peon in a Government Office as far as I recollect, and almost illiterate. The officer who arranged this curious guard was a man named Mackie. Guard duty was a tedious business for someone as tired as me, and I was glad when we were relieved shortly after dawn.

17th December

The officers were clearly duplicating each other's duties and unaware of what duties men had performed the previous day - or even the previous hour. I was collared after breakfast to help bring machine guns from the roof of one of the grandstands, and to build a post with sandbags and get up a Machine Gun as an AA defence.

An unknown officer selected us for this duty, telling us to report to one of the Sergeants somewhere. The post was duly constructed and the MG set up by midday. Sometimes, an officer passing by would take a cursory interest in our work, but no one seemed to have a proprietary interest. Jap planes flew overhead and dropped their bombs now and then. We saw lots of black smoke. From the density, it appeared that an oil installation had been hit. Air-raid alarms sounded constantly and every time they sounded, people threw themselves into a slit trench (of which there were plenty) or laid themselves flat upon the ground well away from any building. We were out in the open in the centre of the race-course and had no need to take these precautions as we could see all planes all around within a mile or two. And so the day passed by.

The evening was quite cheery because a NAAFI canteen was operating on the ground floor of the Turf Club building. I met many men I knew. One of the companies returned from Sitiawan where they had being doing aerodrome defence, but it had been decided to abandon it. I learnt to my dismay that Penang had been evacuated. This accounted for the presence of sailors from the Prince of Wales and the Repulse who had been working on the ferries between Penang and Butterworth (as the regular employees on the ferries had absconded). I heard of one ferry that had been crowded with several hundred passengers. They had all panicked when some Jap planes flew overhead after dropping bombs on Penang. The passengers jumped into the water and my informant said that few, if any, had survived.

Among others, I met Tommy Spence to whom my sister, Lois, was once engaged. Also, Mike Silley, the trainer of a horse that Perry Standish and I had purchased a couple of months ago which we had intended to race in Penang at the New Year races. Silley told me that his wife was going to try to get all the horses taken up Maxwell's Hill in Taiping and let them loose to graze. I heard subsequently that his wife got the horses as far as Kuala Lumpur but was forced to abandon them there.

I also met Bill Harvey, full of beans as ever with an unlimited capacity for beer and talking. I think he was a Company Sergeant Major. Apparently the company that had just returned from Sitiawan contained all the decent fellows, and I regretted that I was not with them.

We had to stand-to during the night but were then allowed to return to bed. We were called up again at about 4 am and ordered to be ready to move in an hour. We remained standing-to until 6.30 when orders were finally given to stand down.

<u>18th December</u>

Breakfast was a poor meal of bread and bacon. After it, I was told to go to the MG post. Several Buffalo aircraft were up in the air at dawn, making off in a Northerly direction, but returning two hours later. No sooner had they landed than several Jap planes appeared - some bombers accompanied by fighters. The bombers dived on the aerodrome and dropped their bombs, and then the whole party made off.

We got an opportunity to fire a hundred rounds or so in the afternoon when a bomber flew about 500 yards above the racecourse to evade a Buffalo. Unfortunately, our gun was a Vickers, and the mounting made it impossible to fire above an angle of 60 degrees. But even so, we could see that the tracer bullets were very close to the target and I think we may have hit it.

Another thrill was the sight of a strange plane being shot down by a Buffalo above the aerodrome about a mile away, but we heard later it was a Dutch plane which had lost its way!

Night fell, and we had another cheerful evening in the canteen.

<u>19th December</u>

We were woken very early with orders to move immediately. It was no false alarm either. We had to evacuate the racecourse to make room for a Regular Regiment. Their transport poured in as we scrambled out. There was much confusion, with orders and counter-orders. I piled into a lorry, and after two miles we stopped and unloaded our kit. We went to sleep on our groundsheets spread on the grass.

Morning revealed that we were in the precincts of a Maternity Hospital. There was a terrific to-do getting transport under cover, and all kit and equipment indoors. By now, our original MG crew of four people had grown into a section consisting of two sergeant-majors, one sergeant and five privates. Two of the privates, including me, knew nothing about machine guns except how to fire them. We saw no officer other than a certain Major Smith. He occasionally gave us an order but never seemed to be quite sure if we were any concern of his.

The two sergeant-majors in my section did not think highly of each other but they tacitly agreed that Sergeant-Major Cameron - a rather uncouth Scottish planter - should be in charge as he was a member of the FMSVF, whereas the other was on attachment as a result of the disbanding of the KVF. We worked all morning digging slit trenches and erecting two MG posts.

The Maternity Hospital was close to the perimeter of the aerodrome, which was non-operational as the RAF had cleared out. However the Japs did not know this and paid the place considerable attention. The result was that we, and the crews of several Lewis guns, were able to let off a few rounds occasionally at the odd bomber as it finished its dive.

The cooking arrangements were decidedly poor and life was rapidly becoming pretty wretched. However, we managed to secure the hospital isolation block for ourselves, and felt quite well off, even to the extent of having a shower of our own. A fairly comfortable night ensued, despite an air-raid false alarm in the darkness and the consequent confusion.

20th December

I woke fully refreshed and took up position on one of the guns - a duty that alternated with periods of resting or digging further and bigger slit trenches - until about 3 o'clock when we again received orders to move. We were allocated a lorry and told to occupy a private house in Racecourse Road.

The house had only recently been vacated by an Ipoh businessman who was also an air-raid warden, or something of the sort. In fact, he returned to the house soon after we moved in and told us we could use anything we found in the house. We had no food, so I rang my brother-in-law Bill Hall who sent someone around with a few tins of food, and the house-boy who was still in residence cooked a couple of chickens. We had plenty of whisky and some beer and soda, and as the refrigerator and wireless were functioning, we managed to make ourselves fairly comfortable.

21st December

Our hopes of enjoying an easy time were rudely shattered early in the morning by orders to move to another house 200 yards away in Brewster Road. We objected strenuously but were told that we were too close to Brigade HQ, and any signs of movement in our compound might bring squadrons of enemy planes on us at any time. So we moved, this time into a very comfortable house. I don't think I have ever known a place so cluttered with blackwood furniture, ivory carvings, chinese porcelain, quaint brassware etc. The place was a veritable museum and its contents must have been of considerable value, but they took up a lot of space and we had always to be careful of breakages. The pantry was literally bursting with food, tinned and otherwise of every description, and there was an ample cellar.

We were certainly in luck, and we greatly resented the intrusion (as we regarded it) later of 7 more volunteers - Lewis gunners. However, we reached an amicable settlement regarding division of food and allotment of sleeping space, but all of us resented it when a section of Malay volunteers also took up residence later in the afternoon. They were led by a very negligible officer named Percival, a schoolmaster in normal life. He apparently made representations about us to Brigade HQ, and was officially told that he could take command of us. We took a dim view of this but just had to get on with it.

We all set to work digging slit trenches and cleaning the guns, relieved by spells of resting. Percival was a very nervous individual and insisted that a guard should be on duty at the gate all night. I did two hours of guard duty.

<u>22nd December</u>

More slit trenches were considered essential first thing next morning - a duty which was carried out until I was detailed mid-morning to go to the Town Hall with a lorry and load up with chairs and benches.

I found other people there doing the same thing, and we all loaded our lorries until the Town Hall was denuded of benches. We were interrupted once by an air-raid alarm and went to a large shelter nearby. The townspeople seemed quite cool and collected. We drove back to the Golf Club and, with the assistance of some Tamil coolies, put all the benches and chairs on the fairways, to deter aircraft landing.

This completed, I returned to quarters and found everyone packing and preparing to move again.

All was bustle and confusion, but at last we got away. We passed my Chrysler near the Golf Club - lying derelict by the side of the road with its tyres slashed. I sighed at the passing of an old and trusted friend. We saw signs of the hasty retreat - dozens of abandoned motor vehicles; ordnance workshops here and there along the road under the rubber trees; a blazing petrol lorry; and an ammunition wagon that had taken the corner too quickly and overturned into a ditch. Pedestrians and cyclists were all loaded with flour, rice or other food

At Kampar we were guided to our billet which was a tin outhouse partly filled with bales of rubber. It was 50 yards from the main road, and about a mile and a half from the village. A Towkay bungalow was about 50 yards further on.

It was quite late when we arrived. We arranged our beds (by this time I had acquired a canvas bed), and we bathed and ate. Again, Percival, whom we had not managed to shake off, ordered that our little section should have its own guard. Accordingly, I did my turn at 6 am the next morning.

<u>23rd December</u>

We had little to do except dig slit trenches. Cooking was a primitive matter and really only consisted of making tea - as our food consisted for the main part of tinned provisions we had brought from our last billet. Percival had no initiative and spent all his time trying to find any superior officer who would give him some orders.

As usual, we had air alarms during the day, but were instructed not to fire at any planes, as we might reveal our whereabouts. The most absurd precautions were taken to conceal packs or machine guns or anything of a military nature, and we all had to paint our tin hats green.

The Towkay's residence nearby was a fairly large one storey wooden building with a covered way attaching it to a pavilion about 40 feet square built in a five acre lake. The lake was an old tin mining excavation, full of clear water and stocked with lots of gold and brown carp. Late in the afternoon, the Towkay decided that the war was too close for comfort and he and his large family - including three wives - departed in two cars and a lorry.

At dusk, I was detailed to take a lorry to Ipoh with another lorry driven by a Malay volunteer, and to report at Brigade HQ which was then in another building in Brewster Road. After a hurried meal, I set out with another volunteer on the seat beside me. We had our rifles handy with one cartridge in the breech and five in the magazine, as there was no knowing whether we would encounter the enemy.

After a few miles, I lost the lights of our rear lorry and had to turn back. We found that it had collided with an army truck going in the opposite direction, and although damage was slight, the escort had received a nasty cut on his forehead, and it looked as if his eye was severely injured. After bandaging the wounded man as best we could, we carried on to Ipoh rather more slowly, without further mishap.

First, we took the injured driver to the Civil Hospital and had him admitted. Then, after a long delay due to difficulty in starting one of the lorries, we found the HQ at about 1 am. We slept in the back of the lorry.

24th December

We were up before dawn and I managed to find something to eat – with some difficulty. The front of the compound was crowded with lorries and cars. There was an order that all vehicles should take cover, which was difficult to comply with, as it had rained during the night. Many cars were bogged down in the flower gardens and lawns. However, after the usual confusion associated with Volunteer moves, some of the lorries were loaded and a convoy proceeded to pick up Brigade and British personnel and impedimenta to head back to Kampar. We discharged our cargo at a coolie line nearby, and I rejoined my section who were weapon-cleaning.

Later that day, I thought that since the Towkay had evacuated his house it might be as well for our section to move in before anyone else had the same idea. I managed to break into the house easily. It was comfortable and well furnished, and although I could find no food or cigarettes, every cupboard was simply bursting with clothes and thousands of dollars worth of perfume, soap cosmetics etc. The womenfolk had clearly decided that war should not deprive them of feminine allurement!

At any rate, we moved in forthwith, and I and another volunteer annexed the pavilion over the lake for ourselves. It was well furnished and spacious, with a double bed and two bathrooms, and the whole pavilion was mosquito-proofed with a fine wire mesh. That night was one of the most comfortable I have ever enjoyed, only marred by having to do guard duty, but, as compensation for my night in Ipoh, I was allowed to do the stint from 9pm to11pm.

The officer, Percival, persisted in living with us. It's a thing no officer should do. Too much association with one's men either breeds familiarity or contempt and dislike.

25th December - Christmas Day

We were again detailed to dig slit trenches and MG positions and left two men behind to cook our midday dinner - and an excellent meal it proved to be. They caught and roasted some of the Towkay's fowls. There were roast potatoes and onions, tomato juice, plum pudding, stewed fruit, champagne brought from Ipoh, and any amount of beer (looted by one of our number from Kampar). After dinner we laid off - washed clothes, and I wrote a letter to Pat. Another comfortable night - apart from guard duty.

26th December

We carried on digging trenches and MG posts and cutting long grass to provide a field of fire. In the afternoon, anyone with jungle experience was invited to join the Gurkhas to go behind enemy lines and harry them (in short, guerilla warfare). I considered joining, but decided I was not in sufficient training for marches of 30 miles per day in jungle, up and down hill. Two people did volunteer, and I was detailed to drive them to Corps HQ in Ipoh.

As far as I could see, neither of them knew much about the jungle - or Malaya. One of them had a broad Somerset accent, and was a dredge-master near Ipoh in ordinary life. The other was a Canadian. He was a better type, but I thought neither would be seen as obvious leaders of men. However, on arrival at Corps HQ, after an interview, they were accepted as suitable candidates.

Driving back through Ipoh, I witnessed dozens of shops being looted by milling natives, squabbling and shouting for desirable articles. I saw one Chinese woman with her face cut open, walking screaming down the street. No police were around and soldiers took no interest in looters other than to keep a passage clear for vehicles.

We called in at Elsie and Bill's house en route to Kampar. It had been stripped of everything of value and it was clear that Bill had evacuated. However, we found a tin of salmon and another of tomato juice, so sat down and had a brief meal. We reached Kampar at dusk, and had a comfortable night - apart from guard duty!

27th December

After another morning of cutting grass and undergrowth, we were told to move into a tumble-down old coolies' quarters over the main road - much to our dismay! But, we just had to make the best of it, and we made ourselves as comfortable as we could in cramped accommodation.

During the day, troops from the British Battalion moved into the area, whilst their officers reconnoitred for defensive positions. I asked one of the few civilians around to post a letter to Pat. This was strictly against orders as all our letters were supposed to be censored by our officer (Percival). He, by the way, still clung to us, persisting in sleeping with us, instead of with the other officers or by himself in dignified solitude, as he could easily have done. He also had his meals with us.

28th December

The day was spent carrying barbed wire up steep hills at the back of the Chinese cemetery, erecting triple dannert fences over ridges to protect MG posts there, and clearing lines of fire for machine guns. A number of valleys and tracks were also fenced off to deter entry by the enemy. The British Battalion set up their HQ in a 30 acre block of rubber opposite the cemetery, surrounding it with triple dannert.

The Malay volunteers were lazy and incompetent and shirked any labour. They completely disgusted me. I thought it was only a matter of time before they would have to be discarded, and so it proved. Desertions by Malays took place daily, and most took their arms with them.

It was clear that the Japs anticipated a stand would be made at Kampar because, apart from bombing the railway station (which they did pretty effectively), planes were constantly overhead. They were studying all troop movements and military activity around Kampar carefully. It must have been fairly obvious to them what was going on, even though pains were taken to conceal all traces of digging etc.

I saw Tony Willis of the 22nd Mountain Regiment and decided to ask if they had a vacancy for a survey officer. I felt it was absurd for me to be doing work that could be done by anyone - if my talents (such as they were) could be better used.

All in all, it was a very wearing day and I was glad to get to bed.

29th December

I was sent off with a lorry and escort early in the morning to pick up labour from a mine seven miles north of Kampar. No-one was around when I arrived, so I scoured the neighbourhood and I managed to get 20 Chinese to come back with me, promising them $2 per day and appealing to their aid in preventing the Japanese from winning the war. Back at Kampar, they were given tools and led off to dig and clear undergrowth - similar to the work I had been doing for the past few days.

I had spotted a sound-looking lorry behind a shed which appeared to be in good order when we were looking for the labour. So, we returned to the mine to pick up this lorry. We also picked up 20 Tamil coolies and drove back to Kampar, handing the lorry over to the Transport Officer. In all, about 200 coolies were collected for defensive works that day. I think many carried on working, but in diminishing numbers each day, until the battle finally commenced.

During the afternoon, I and another volunteer were ordered to join a rifle platoon, so we went back to the coolie lines to collect our kit. The lorry failed to turn up, so we obeyed orders and waited. I reviewed my kit which now consisted of two kit bags and one small suitcase. I dumped a lot and put the rest into one kit bag. We found a couple of tins of pineapple and some bully in the coolie lines, and washed it all down with water. We settled down to sleep and woke feeling quite fresh, even though grubby and dirty.

30th December

On waking, we decided it was no use waiting any longer, and we got a lift in a lorry to platoon HQ in the school building. Apparently we had been forgotten by Lt Mackie, the platoon commander.

After a sketchy breakfast, we marched to a Chinese hut outside the perimeter and left our kit there. We marched to the Chinese cemetery on the opposite side of the road from Batallion HQ, and dug fire trenches all day - most tiring work in the boiling sun and no rests.

When night fell, the platoon returned to the hut, and after some food we were given explicit instructions not to speak loudly nor allow lights to be seen. We were forbidden even to smoke out of doors.

Suddenly there was a stampede outside, and it was whispered that the enemy were all around. We were told to rendezvous immediately at some point outside, but the night was pitch dark and no-one knew where the rendezvous point was. Our organisation rapidly deteriorated and it was a wonder no-one was shot. We all mistook trees for the enemy and challenged each other. Several men swore they had seen figures who when challenged did not reply. No-one knew what the situation was, and to cap it all, our platoon commander had disappeared.

After a little while, word went around that it was all a false alarm, and order was once more created out of chaos. Then, the platoon commander re-appeared. Apparently, when the alarm was given he had dashed off to Battalion HQ for orders but had not told anyone!

I well remember my guard duty that night, from 4 to 6 am. One's imagination plays funny tricks on one's eyes and ears, and I was glad when my turn was over.

31st December

After breakfast, we carried on excavations in the cemetery. It was quite usual to dig up human bones. The trenches were hidden from the air by trees, so it was aggravating to be told to cover all exposed earth with turf or green leaves. Bombs were dropped now and then in the vicinity, but none near us.

I had written a chit a day or two previously, forwarded by the OC British Battalion to the OC 22nd Mountain Regiment, asking if he had any use for my services. Today, the Adjutant of the Mountain Regiment came around and told me that the Colonel would very much like to have me as survey officer. It would have to be sanctioned by Command and he had forwarded my letter accordingly. All I could do was wait.

Orders were read, including one from Corps Commander that there was to be no question of a withdrawal. The Kampar position was to be defended at all costs - last man and last round. I must confess, on hearing this, I felt a thrill of apprehension.

Road traffic was extremely heavy - mainly towards the south. Two anti-tank guns were in position between the cemetery and Battalion HQ. Two batteries of 25 pounders each were preparing gun positions about 400 yards south of us - and maybe there were more guns further south. Taken by and large, it looked as if battle was imminent.

Ever since evacuating Ipoh, fires could be seen glowing at all points of the compass. On the afternoon Ipoh was evacuated, I had seen an enormous pillar of smoke which coiled slowly within itself and expanded outward and upward until it appeared to tower above the world. There was no wind, and the smoke increased in density and remained in situ until night fell. It transpired that this was the result of the bombing of an ammunition train.

Food was brought to us in our trench at meal times. As the afternoon wore on, we gathered that the intermittent explosions, which appeared to be approaching, were actually our demolition parties blowing bridges between Kampar and Ipoh. At nightfall, we were warned of the possibility of enemy attack and the importance of not revealing our whereabouts.

It was impossible to sleep in the trenches with myriads of mosquitoes. At 9 pm, the stillness was broken without warning by the thunder of the 25 pounders behind us. This carried on for an hour or two with no reply from the enemy, and then all was quiet again. Those of us trying to snatch a few minutes sleep despite the ravages of the mosquitoes, were wakened and told to keep bayonets fixed and five cartridges in the magazines of our rifles. Everyone was on edge with excitement, but I think our officer had unwittingly exaggerated the seriousness of the situation. It was unlikely the enemy could penetrate our outer defences on such a black night and if he had tried, he would certainly have been discovered.

<u>1st January 1942</u>

Dawn was a relief. Tired and filthy as we were, it was wonderful to stretch our cramped limbs by marching back along the road to the gun battery. We sat under the rubber trees and ate our food, washing it down with water from our water bottles.

Enemy aircraft were active, viciously dive-bombing all likely looking patches of trees that might conceal the 25 pounder guns. There were some air-raid shelters nearby, and we were most grateful for them. The bombs fell all around us.

At about 10 o'clock, our platoon commander received orders to prevent the enemy infiltrating to our east. We proceeded through the rubber and around a hillside. Rifle fire was becoming pretty general, and we thought the enemy was very close. It was only later that I found out that nearly all rifle-fire was at trees and bushes that imagination had magnified into enemies.

In the distance we could see figures in a valley around some Chinese squatters' houses, but could not tell who they were. We could also see figures on the opposite hillside - but again too far away to distinguish whether they were friends or enemies.

A soldier from the British Battalion came running up the hillside towards us, quite incoherent and practically naked. He had thrown his rifle away, apparently scared out of his wits. Someone took him to Battalion HQ.

It was clear that the enemy was not far away because mortar shells began to fly over our heads. Some exploded in the tree-tops. On the whole, things were rather unpleasant. However, at about 2 o'clock, rifle and mortar fire in our immediate vicinity ceased and we returned to Battalion HQ, near the huts we had recently occupied. After some lunch we dug trenches. We were sheltered by a hill from gunfire from the north or aircraft overhead, so when the job was done we were able to wash and shave and clean our rifles etc.

Later in the afternoon, we reconnoitred a good section post, overlooking a ditch with a dry bottom, about 300 yards north of our huts. It was an excellent defensive position, being about two feet deep overgrown by grass and ferns on either side.

Enemy planes were doing their best to destroy the batteries and HQ. But, with excellent cover from the rubber and well camouflaged guns, they did no damage - though at times they must have flown as low as 1,000 feet. Casualties began to trickle in, and ambulances took them away to Advance Dressings Stations and Casualty Clearing Stations.

At dusk, we withdrew to a position within the Battalion HQ perimeter wire. We were given a covered dug-out to sleep in. It was most uncomfortable with barely enough room to kneel, although eighteen of us had to sleep in it. A section of perimeter wire was allocated to patrol each night and, being short, we had to do two spells of one hour each. The wire was hung with empty tins which would rattle if the wire was shaken - to provide advance warning of any intruder.

The guns put up a terrific barrage for half an hour or so. After that, there was dead silence until 5 am when the guns commenced a perfect thunder of noise - carrying on for about two hours. We heard later that a concentration of Jap forces had been observed, apparently preparing for a dawn attack and our artillery barrage had inflicted enormous casualties on them. It was also reported that the artillery had done some good shooting on a bridge just as two tanks were about to cross.

2nd January

Towards dawn, between bursts of artillery fire, we could hear continuous machine gun and rifle fire, and it was obvious that an attack was being repelled. Apparently the barbed wire we had put up on the hillsides had turned out to be of some value as it had stemmed the tide of a Jap dawn attack and allowed our four machine guns to inflict deadly casualties on the enemy when they tried to cut through the wire.

My section was given a trench, covered with boards and a foot of earth on top. It was virtually an air-raid shelter but with a lateral aperture about 2 feet high screened with bushes and facing the enemy.

Enemy planes raided our lines all day, paying particular attention to the guns, which fired only occasionally. They were concealed extremely well. Each time a plane came within range it received a peppering from machine guns, Lewis guns and rifles, and although the results were not spectacular there were probably many hits. One plane, at least, was brought down by small arms fire. The few Bofors AA guns we had originally had disappeared, and of course none of our planes had been seen since Ipoh. The weather was perfect, which was something to be thankful for - because to have endured all this in rainy weather would have been misery! Mortar fire increased as the day progressed and seemed to be mainly directed at the rubber, under which HQ and resting and wounded troops sheltered. Unfortunately we had no mortars to return fire.

At mid-day, I saw movement on a hillside about four miles away, and through field glasses I could see a few figures working in the vicinity of a house, and other figures about

200 yards away. The second in command of the British Battalion was summoned and after a long look he decided to ask the gunner to put down some gunfire on that locality. After 15 minutes, the firing started, and although the first two shells fell short, the next were closer, and after that they fell all around the target. The bottom floor of the house could not be seen as some high land obscured it, but the firing certainly accelerated the movement of all the people in the neighbourhood. Although I couldn't say for certain that they were Japs, it was definitely a congregation of numbers of people, and may well have been a Jap HQ.

As the day progressed, machine gun fire grew less, as a result of withdrawals, and rifle fire increased in volume and bullets began to whistle past unpleasantly. The hollow "pong" of mortar shells, together with an accompanying whistle and short sharp explosions, quickened in the rate of fire. Taken by and large, it was evident the enemy was unpleasantly close and all around us.

One sniper had found a comfortable position in a tree where he had been able to pick off a dozen of our men before he was discovered. We knew of their great skill in using camouflage, and every clump of grass and every tree within half a mile was subjected to close inspection now and then.

At 5 o'clock, I suddenly saw five men carrying heavy objects along the pipeline fringing our ditch. They appeared to be Chinese, but no Chinese would remain in no-man's land longer than it took him to get out of it, so they were clearly not Chinese, and if they were, they were up to no good. I could see that they were not our troops. I quickly asked the NCO's permission to fire but he, cautious and frightened soul, refused. I was in no doubt it was a Jap mortar party wearing Chinese clothes - a ruse resorted to by them almost invariably during the war.

At about 6.30, just before dark, the firing died away until only an occasional 'pop' was heard, and it was then that the orders came through that all forces would withdraw from Kampar at 10.30. We vacated our trench almost immediately. A number of the volunteers were nervous wrecks by this time, mainly as a result of age and loss of sleep, allied to unaccustomed physical labour, so it was arranged that they should be taken by lorry together with our kit to a rear position.

All the belongings I possessed, apart from those in my haversack, were in one kit bag. It was loaded onto a lorry and I never saw it again.

From dusk onwards, HQ was the scene of quiet and well-organised activity. There was no moon, and the only lights were occasional glimmers of a few cigarettes (smoked against orders). Men were withdrawn silently and swiftly from outposts; signal wire was reeled in; and all unnecessary equipment and men were sent off to the rear as soon as lorries were available. By 9 o'clock, only a few hundred men remained, and practically all transport had disappeared.

My platoon was ordered to take up a position 300 yards south of Battalion HQ on the main road to cover the withdrawal of the rearmost anti-tank gun. Then followed some of the most eerie moments of my life. Filing along the main road in complete silence and in intense darkness; receiving and obeying orders given in a whisper to lie down in the ditch with rifles loaded and bayonets fixed. We knew that there was nothing between the enemy and ourselves, and for all we knew, he might be only a few yards away and about to attack. Or, a tank with lights blazing and all guns firing might suddenly appear from around the corner.

We waited tensely in complete silence, lying in the ditches on either side of the road with our rifles firmly clutched in our hands and pointing approximately down the road. After about 15 minutes, a heavy Marmon-Harrington lorry rumbled up in reverse. In a minute, the anti-tank gun we were covering was hitched on, and the lorry and gun sped off. We rose on the whispered word of command and returned to outside HQ where the remainder of our force was lined up on the road. At the command - again given in a whisper passed on from unit to unit - we marched down the road, keeping to the grass verge as much as possible.

As we continued, various small units of men, who in their turn had been covering our withdrawal, joined the column. After a mile or two, as we carried on at a brisk pace, we realised that the withdrawal had been carried out without a hitch in a most efficient manner, and that the enemy were quite unaware of the retreat. Otherwise, there is no doubt that they would have done all in their power to prevent it and to turn our orderly withdrawal into a flight.

During our march along the road, we passed a number of anti-tank guns and demolition parties at work on bridges. The number of bridges on which preparations for demolition were proceeding seemed to me to be surprisingly few.

That night, we marched about 8 miles and I think it was about 1 o'clock when we stopped. We were dog-tired and told to rest. We lay flat on our backs and slept straightaway - only to be awakened half an hour later and marched another mile to lorries which drove us a further 20 miles. On arrival, each man was given a plateful of bully beef stew (a disgusting mess!) and a mug of tea. At about 3.30 am we were allowed to sleep on the ground.

CHAPTER 3

Transfer to the Mountain Regiment

3rd January

In the morning, we were allowed to rest and bathe and wash our clothes, as there was a small brook in the vicinity. The rain came down in torrents in the afternoon. There was no shelter, as we were in a rubber estate and there were no buildings nearby. Our platoon commander, Mackie, took leave of us during the day and Longmore, a sergeant, took his place. Mackie apparently had fever and was being sent to the rear.

A splinter that had run into my arm a day or two earlier began to worry me and I visited the RAP, but the doctor said it would be OK in a day or two and did nothing.

By Jove, it was a treat to be free from the sounds of gunfire and constant explosions. We revelled in it. But our hopes for a good night's sleep were soon dashed. After a march of 5 miles we had to pile into lorries again and proceed south in convoy at slow speed. The lorries were confoundedly uncomfortable, as they were crammed with arms and equipment, and we could doze only for a minute or two at a time. We arrived at our destination at about 1 am, and our section was billeted in a small dirty Chinese squatter's hut. Other units were similarly housed, or otherwise just lay on the ground and slept.

4th January

We stood-to at 6 am and, immediately after breakfast (a poor meal of bread and butter and some tinned fish), we were told that we had to cover a withdrawal of Punjabi and Gurkha troops.

Apart from my haversack, rifle and 100 rounds, I had to carry a Lewis gun which got confoundedly heavy after two miles. I exchanged it for two panniers, each containing 4 cylinders of ammunition, which were also very heavy, or seemed to be after a while.

We occupied a position on a hillside overlooking a main road, enabling us to fire at any enemy approaching through the rubber. Half the platoon remained on guard whilst the other half rested. When night fell, two sentries were posted and changed each hour about 80 yards ahead of our position. Again pitch darkness and that eerie feeling of not knowing when or how the enemy might attack. We were relieved to hear the troops whose withdrawal we were covering, retiring along the main road, and at about 11 pm we too withdrew to the main road.

After marching with heavy loads for 2 to 3 miles, we found lorries waiting to convey us to our next halt, which turned out to be near the Shin river. We slept on the ground again under cover of rubber.

5th January

Again we rested and were able to shave and bathe once more. I couldn't change my clothes, as I had no spare clothing of any description. We could hear bomb blasts at intervals during the day, and learnt that it was enemy bombing directed at the Shin river-bridge. The whole battalion was under heavy rubber and we could not even see the sky, but every now and then planes flew overhead - Jap, of course, for we had given up hope of any support from our own planes.

My arm had swollen considerably and was very painful. An orderly at the RAP performed what he called an 'aspiratory operation' on it. This consisted of plunging a hypodermic syringe needle three quarters of an inch into my arm and sucking out some pus. This gave some relief, but the pain grew much worse soon after.

At dusk, we were ordered into lorries. We heard that the Japs had landed at Kuala Selangor and were going to force us down the Peninsula. During the long, tedious and uncomfortable journey, the pain in my arm became almost unbearable. My right hand had swollen so much that I couldn't grasp my rifle. On de-bussing I pointed this out to Longmore who ordered me to stay with the lorries, because in my condition I would be a drag on the unit. I got back into one of the lorries, which belonged to an Australian Transport Unit, and found that they were going to a rendezvous near Rawang. There was nothing for it but to accompany them, and finding a stretcher in the lorry, I lay on it and immediately went to sleep.

6th January

I woke at 7 o'clock, in one of fifteen lorries parked in a European rubber estate. Everyone was asleep and appeared to be very comfortable. I was the exception, as by now the pain in my arm was intense. It was swollen and inflamed.

The Australian drivers provided me with a meal and then dropped me off at a Casualty Clearing Station about 15 miles from Kuala Lumpur.

My arm was in a bad way, and I had a large swelling in my armpit too. The Medical Officer ("MO") in charge opened up the swelling, releasing a lot of pus, and put on a hot fomentation. This gave me great relief!

The Indian orderlies told me that wounded had been coming in all day. The usual procedure with the wounded was to obtain full particulars, including name and unit, and write it on a piece of paper and pin it to his coat. He would be relieved of weapons and equipment; his wounds dressed; any necessary surgical aid given; and then sent on as quickly as possible to a Base Hospital in Kuala Lumpur.

The MO told me that the British Battalion were at Batu Berjuntai, 25 miles away. A WO was going to deliver some medical supplies and would take me with him. I was very relieved to hear this, as it would have been difficult to get back otherwise.

The hospital provided me with a good dinner and a comfortable stretcher to sleep on. I enjoyed the sleep although it was disturbed by ambulances rolling up at intervals bringing in wounded.

<u>7th January</u>

Early in the morning, a British Officer of the Dogras was brought in wounded. He had been shot in the stomach and his stretcher was filled with blood. He was quite conscious and cheerful. Once his wounds had been dressed he was sent on, but the MO told me that he could not possibly last more than 24 hours.

Another Dogra officer with bullet wounds in his chest was brought in, and so were lots of Indian soldiers with wounds of varying degrees of seriousness from bullets and mortar-bombs. They were all casualties from the Batu Berjuntai area, where the British Battalion was now in action - which I was about to rejoin.

The Eurasian WO and I set off by car after lunch, following a tortuous route. We had to consult the road-map frequently. We turned off the main Kuala Selangor road on to a back-road which, according to the map, was a direct route to our destination. After a while, we began to doubt the map, as it was almost entirely through jungle. The possibility of running into a Jap patrol crossed my mind. We passed safely through Batu Berjuntai, but during the next two miles, we had to pull up several times under trees at the side of the road when enemy planes flew low overhead.

During one such halt, I saw a British officer nearby in the rubber. I called out to him to find out the where my Battalion was. As luck would have it, it turned out to be Guy Cowie, who was commanding the 22nd Mountain Regiment in the absence of the Colonel who was in Singapore (having his piles attended to). Guy was keen to secure my services, and I said I was sure that a chit from him to Clive Wallace, adjutant of the British Battalion, would release me.

He immediately wrote out the chit and I took it directly to Clive, who, as it happened, was not more than 400 yards away at Battalion HQ in a defensive position in an oil palm estate. All cars and lorries in the vicinity were well camouflaged with bushes and palm fronds. I was warned about being seen from the air, as enemy bombers had been extremely active all day - bombing anything that moved. Although planes were flying very low, they were not fired at for fear of giving away our position.

Clive agreed to my transfer immediately, so I handed over my rifle, kit, and iron rations. I went over to my old platoon to say au revoir. It had amalgamated with another platoon by this time but was down to just 20 men as a result of sickness. Longmore was still in charge.

I returned to the area where I had met Guy and found a small hut which was serving as Regimental HQ. Two or three staff cars and a Signal wagon were parked nearby. I met Peters, the Signal Officer; a European Signal sergeant; Tony Willis, the adjutant; Dizzy Coleman, the assistant adjutant, who I had not met before; and the CO, Major Guy Cowie. They all made me very welcome, telling me that my knowledge of the country would be invaluable in addition to my services as Survey officer (as the Regiment had no survey expert). I was delighted to hear all this, and felt relief to be with social equals again. The Volunteers had been good fellows, but there were not many of them that I would have been able to present to Pat as friends.

At 6 pm, the signal cable was reeled in and the signal apparatus packed and Dizzy and I drove to a bungalow which was being used as a mess. It now became the Regiment HQ as the Signals section connected up the telephone cables linking us with the two batteries in position in the vicinity and with Brigade HQ. Salvoes of gunfire heralded nightfall and then complete silence fell, broken only by the rumbling of lorries (most military transport was at night for obvious reasons).

At the bungalow I met Nehtu, the Regimental MO, a charming and cultured young Indian (a Hindu). He applied hot water fomentations to my arm which was in a bad state, and dressed it properly. We then had a hearty meal and I thoroughly enjoyed a comfortable bed. It was a congenial environment and a complete contrast to life in the previous few weeks. I felt happier than at any time since leaving Pat.

8th January

Up early. An ample breakfast served by Indian orderlies. My arm was again dressed by the MO, and then Guy took me to 4 Battery. It was cleverly camouflaged on the edge of the rubber estate about 500 yards from the bungalow. One section was manned by Sikhs, the other by Punjabi Mussalmen. Lieutenant James explained a plotting board and other artillery technicalities to me, including how to load and fire the howitzers. All very interesting!

Returning from the guns, I saw Major Perry Standish and Lieutenant Drummond Black enjoying a mug of beer outside their mess wagon which was a most ingenious contrivance. They invited me to join them. The vehicle had been a bus, but all the seats had been removed and the interior had been fitted with lockers and cupboards which, I was assured, contained sufficient food and drink of every conceivable kind to last the Mess for months. I gathered that this stock had been acquired from various sources without any monetary outlay, as a result of DB's initiative. The van contained a refrigerator and was fitted inside with electric light. It had sufficient room to allow four officers to sit in comfort around a table inside. In short, it was apparent that the officers believed in fighting this war in comfort. And who would blame them?

I was told to go to Rawang with Dizzy Coleman - to reconnoitre and select a suitable harbour for all our vehicles, and to see if a particular road from Kuang to Rawang was passable. It wasn't, but we carried on to Rawang, eating our lunch on the way (beer, sardines, cheese and biscuits). Most of the area was already occupied but we found a suitable spot two miles north of Rawang and we returned to HQ at dusk.

During our absence, orders had been received for the Regiment (consisting of three batteries) to be ready to move at 10 pm. We got to Rawang at about 4 am and slept in the vehicles until dawn.

9th January

During the morning, Regimental HQ was ordered to join up with 15 Brigade HQ on the opposite side of the Rawang river, under some rubber. We were bombed in the process. A Signal lorry which stopped whilst the occupants ran for cover was machine-gunned and received several bullets through the instrument panel.

The battle on the main front got nearer during the day and again the air activity was intense. Enemy planes flew only a hundred feet or so overhead, but although they bombed and machine-gunned all around our patch of rubber, we escaped severe attention.

My duties at Brigade HQ included setting up and manning 3 Lewis gun posts with HQ personnel and inspecting the posts occasionally. The Subadar Major however was most efficient and I left most of this work to him.

Stories of 5th column activities had been circulating freely since hostilities began and the initial defeat of our forces at Jitra was attributed in no small degree to assistance given by Malays to the enemy. There had been instances of active participation in the fighting by Malays and Tamils, and we were warned to look out for signals from the ground to enemy aircraft by mirrors, planks or logs laid on the ground, or strips of cloth, or even swathes cut in the grass in the form of arrow-heads pointing to a target. Flags of white cloth also held some significance.

The Doctor was asked to act as an interpreter in the cross-examination of some Tamils who were alleged to have signalled to aircraft near Brigade HQ. The upshot was that some of the suspects were shot forthwith and the village to which they belonged was fired.

I spent the night in a staff car and slept quite well.

<u>10th January</u>

During the day, I drafted my application for a commission which the adjutant typed out and forwarded to the CRA for transmission to the right quarters.

At 2 o'clock, we received orders for 15 Brigade to withdraw by the west road out of Rawang to Kuang, avoiding the main Rawang-KL road as it was enemy country.

By 3 o'clock, all HQ vehicles had left, apart from two staff cars, one for the CO and Adjutant and the other for Lt Peters (the Signal Officer) and myself. Just outside Rawang we were machine-gunned by 3 Jap dive bombers. We had to jump out and fling ourselves into the roadside ditches. The cars were undamaged and none of us was hit. Then ensued a wild drive through no-man's-land. We had to stop three times whilst Jap planes flew overhead. It was with some relief that we reached Kuang. Our engine seized just after arrival, but after thoroughly dousing it with buckets of cold water and re-filling with oil, it began to function satisfactorily again and gave no further trouble.

We carried on our way to KL followed by 4 Battery who just got through before the leading Jap troops came up. En route, we observed smoke from many large fires. We were apparently putting a scorched-earth policy into operation. But all the fires were dwarfed by an enormous blaze and pillar of black smoke near KL from millions of gallons of burning oil stocks.

Arriving in KL, we found that RHQ transport had already gone ahead of us to Seramban, to pitch camp about 3 miles out of the town. Peters and I had a hard job finding them. Our orders were to bring the vehicles to Laku, but it was late and the roads were congested with vehicles of every description, so we thought it best for Peters to go on to Laku and for me to stay the night. The Doctor was delighted to see us. He and I had an excellent meal with a bottle or two of iced lager and he arranged a sleeping place in a Chinese hut - all of which was much appreciated.

<u>11th January</u>

I was up before dawn, and an hour or two later rejoined the the remainder of RHQ in an Estate manager's bungalow just south of Laku. I had nothing to do all day, so I read any literature I could find about artillery. The owner of the bungalow had obviously left in great haste and although there was nothing left of value, there was a quite decent Philco radio with a battery, which Peters immediately installed in his car. It was in constant use thereafter and proved a boon. I acquired shorts, shirts and boots from the quartermaster. In the house, I picked up several other useful articles such as soap and hair-oil. I also acquired a revolver, binoculars, compass and map-case which had belonged to Major Scott, who had been killed at Batu Berjuntai by a sniper just before my arrival.

The day was unbroken by incident, except for frequent alarms and enemy planes flying overhead. I had a good night's sleep in a pukka bed with a mosquito net.

12th January

I woke very refreshed and had a warm bath and shave in comfort.

Guy Cowie asked me to accompany him to Brigade HQ which was in the open and under rubber, near the village of Laku. At 3.30pm, I was ordered to join a recce party to go to Tangkak to select suitable harbours for the whole regiment.

I took the office recce truck with Corporal Horsman and a Sikh driver. We picked up Tony Trench* from 4 Battery. I led, as I knew the way, followed by two other cars with representatives of 7,10, and 21 Batteries. I recollect that the truck was fairly heavy as we had quite a lot of beer on board. Earlier in the morning word had been received that Fraser & Neave was distributing beer gratis to anyone who wanted it and I had sent two lorries which both returned loaded. We gave half to the Sikhs in RHQ and half of the remainder to the Signal sections, keeping the rest at RHQ. Mess is always called on for a lot of hospitality.

* after the war, Tony Trench was Headmaster of Eton

We were able to make good time, with little traffic. We had several Sepoys with us, and left them at salient corners to act as traffic policemen for the main convoy, which we knew would depart half an hour after us but would not be able to maintain our pace. We reckoned it would arrive three hours after us.

On the road from Tampin to Jasin, it was hard to realise that a war was in progress. All was peaceful, and villagers were unperturbed - at least outwardly. However, Jasin itself was full of troops. Some Civil Defence officials were stupidly officious about our lights which they said didn't conform to regulations. We soon settled them and carried on to Tangkak, where by chance we met a staff captain in the RA, who was able to tell us about our intended harbour, which saved a lot of time.

We left a guide at Tangkak and carried on to Tangkak Estate about 12 miles further on. Practically all the rubber on both sides of the road was already occupied by withdrawing or reserve troops. Their locations were indicated by lamp-illuminated unit signs. These signs were supposed to be shaded but most of them were not and must have been visible from the air.

On Tangkak Estate, we found a large brick Manager's bungalow on a hill surrounded by lawns on which grew some large shade trees. The rubber grew to the edges of the lawn on gently undulating country. We inspected the area by torchlight to assess how many vehicles could be accommodated and whether a quick getaway would be possible. All unit representatives got together and agreed on the parking of vehicles. This done, we opened up the bungalow and made billeting arrangements. We appreciated a glass or two of beer or whisky and soda (of which we carried plentiful supplies) in comfort, together with a chunk of bread and some bully beef or salmon.

We expected the Regiment to arrive at midnight and waited for them by the side of the road. Each person was ready to guide his particular unit to its allotted parking space. The convoy was a little late, but by 4 am every vehicle was in harbour and under cover. I think we numbered about 160 vehicles in total.

Indian troops are much more adaptable than British, and by the time the last vehicle was parked everyone else had eaten their haversack rations and were asleep. In an artillery regiment, tents or other accommodation were not necessary, as each vehicle averaged only six or seven men.

13th January

After a couple of hours sleep on a settee in the bungalow sitting-room, I supervised the camouflage of HQ's vehicles and got various lorries under cover. Detachments went out to repair and pick up lorries that had fallen by the wayside during the night.

During the morning, some Chinese were brought in who could not speak English. They had been arrested by some of our troops who thought they were behaving in a suspicious way. I questioned them in Malay and they told me they were communist organisers who had the blessing of the military authorities in Singapore who had furnished them with special passports. This story was most likely true. It was at about this time that the Military were making use of the Communists as belligerents and for espionage.

However, I was unaware of this at the time, and I advised Guy to send them to Divisional HQ for further questioning.

I decided to take some sheets and pillowslips and two cushions from the bungalow. It was a fortunate acquisition, as they came in very useful and I still have them.

We received orders for a withdrawal in the evening, and again I was sent ahead with the same reconnaissance party. Progress to Segamat was uneventful without much traffic. Some officers wanted to send letters. The Post Office was functioning, as were the Police. This was the first sign of Police activity I had seen since leaving Ipoh. Of course everyone in Johore thought that the front line was still at Kuala Selangor - thinking that the war would not reach them for months - if ever.

En route to Labis, I remembered the Gennang club on whose padang I had played rugger in 1928 and suggested a visit to the other officers, who were enthusiastic. The club was only 100 yards from the main road. When we drew up outside I saw, to my disappointment, that some Australian troops were already billeted there. The club was bare of drinks, but it crossed my mind that it might have a storeroom.

The door to the store was downstairs in a most obscure place, and in a few minutes we managed to open it. It was packed with all sorts of drinks: spirits, wines, liqueurs, cases of beer and soft drinks. We loaded our car with what we could carry and went on our way - stopping in Labis for coffee and something to eat, and to buy electric torches, razor blades and other oddments. It was raining by this time, coming down in torrents.

At Chaah, we waited for the staff captain, but there was no sign of him, and so we piled out of our cars and waited on the verandah of a shop. It was a rainy-cold afternoon and clearly a glass or two of beer was indicated! So we passed the time until 6 pm, when we decided that we should push on and try to get any harbour for the night near Kluang, as the Regiment must by now be on its way. One of the staff cars stayed at Chaah to inform the CO, and the other two carried on.

The road was very dangerous because lorries without lights were parked on the side of the road in odd places. The night was pitch black and the rain was torrential. As we got closer to Yong Peng, the traffic increased and the confusion in the village was colossal. To add to the confusion, there was flood water about a foot deep at the road junction. I knew the district in 1928/29 and had thought it would be easy to find a good harbour near Kluang. But all space near the roadside was already taken up, as the unit signs indicated. Then I remembered the Lambak Estate, and we set out with renewed hope. The manager was in his bungalow and very surprised to find the war almost on his doorstep. He accompanied us in our search for a suitable harbour and we found one with no difficulty. We accepted a drink from him and after a few minutes returned to get in touch with the Regiment.

Rain was still pelting down. Tony Trench, Corporal Horsman, the driver and I took turns to drive. After a while one felt an almost irresistible inclination to sleep. The on-coming traffic got thicker and thicker. A few miles north of Yong Peng it became an unbroken line and impossible to get past, because cars kept cutting in. I have never seen such a traffic jam - all on a narrow road with ditches either side.

Fortunately, at this point we met some Regimental lorries and found that the convoy had broken up. A short while later, the CO turned up. We learnt from him that all traffic arrangements had been thrown into complete chaos by the advance of Australian units into Segamat to take over from 11 Division. He told us that he had heard of an excellent harbour back in the Oil Palm Plantations estate.

We turned round with some difficulty and took our place in the procession which eventually became less congested. The road was comparatively clear by the time we reached Kluang, and we reached our destination about dawn. Guides had been posted en route, and as the rain had cleared by now, all lorries had either arrived in the Oil Palm estate or were otherwise accounted for.

We made a quick reconnaissance of the estate, which was just a maze of roads. Areas were allocated to each battery and to HQ. The reconnaissance work was made much easier by using a map of the estate which the manager had given us.

I had met the manager, whose name was Gibson, several years before. He gave us every assistance, putting a large vacant bungalow at our disposal as well as offering to billet the officers of 7 and 21 Batteries in his own house which was spacious and luxuriously fitted. Other officers messed in the Assistant's bungalow which was also quite spacious but not so modern, constructed of wood.

14th January

Detachments of the LAD were sent out early to assist the stragglers, and by evening all transport had turned up safely.

During the day, floods of instructions were received concerning the morale of troops and the necessity for smartening up and close-order drill.

Accommodation for the troops was not good, but they made themselves as comfortable as they could - in and under wagons and in tents and odd buildings - and were quite content. Our own messing arrangements were quite good. Although I did not have a bed, I slept in comparative comfort on the floor of a bedroom which I shared with Tony Trench and Athol Long.

I noticed that Gibson seemed most perturbed by the military situation. By the evening, he, his Engineer and their womenfolk had quit the Estate.

To my delight, I got through to Pat on the Military Exchange for a few minutes at midday. She said she was well. I could not tell her where I was speaking from, but said that I hoped to be able to get to Singapore within a few days. 11 Division was now resting. Its Advance HQ was at Ayer Hitam and its Rear HQ at Rengam.

15th January

I spent the morning making several copies of the plan of the Estate. In the afternoon I heard that the Johore Volunteer Engineers were in the neighbourhood, so I decided to see if I could contact Jack Crosse. I found the JVE HQ without much difficulty, in a harbour near Kluang. Jack was not there, but I met Eddie, who was his 2nd in command (rank of Captain), and had a glass of beer with him. The JVE had been mobilised since the outbreak of hostilities and were attached to the Australians doing odd jobs, such as demolition and construction of tank traps.

Guy told me that he was sending Freddie (Capt) Cross to Singapore tomorrow, to bring back reinforcements, and that I could go with him. This was terrific news, and every minute seemed to drag until I could be with my beloved wife again.

16th January

We set off early in a recce truck accompanied by four empty lorries in which to bring back the reinforcements. The journey to Singapore was uneventful. It was a beautiful day and I enjoyed seeing the countryside in which I had spent my first year in Malaya, and I noted the great changes that had taken place. I saw a flourishing estate of healthy well-grown rubber on land which I had surveyed personally when it had been covered with dense jungle - my first job in Malaya!

The road was full of military traffic. Occasionally, cars loaded with household paraphernalia would pass by at breakneck speed. They were natives evacuating in a hurry - trying to save what they could from the wreckage of their homes.

Arriving in Singapore, we went straight to the reinforcement camp - through Bukit Timah and Serangoon along the Tampenis Road where, with some difficulty, we located the camp in a rubber estate. We left the lorries there and arranged to pick up the reinforcements in two days time. We then drove to Eden Hall.

Pat was out when I got to Eden Hall* but it was a joy to be

* See Appendix 2 re Eden Hall

welcomed into this cool, dignified, and well-run home. Auntie May and Uncle Eze were there and gave me a warm homecoming. They told me that Mum and Aunt Trilby had left for Australia the previous week with Elsie's two children. Apparently neither of them could stand the bombing. Poor Mum in particular was in a dreadful state. In the ARP shelter she always used to smother her head in cushions whenever bomb explosions could be heard.

Pat and Elsie were working in the Blood transfusion Centre at the General Hospital. They had been doing this work for the past few weeks, apart from the couple of days that Pat had spent in hospital as a patient and a few days subsequent convalescence.

Uncle Eze invited Freddie to stay at Eden Hall, and after a hearty lunch, Freddie and I retired to our respective rooms for a siesta. After a nap, a hot bath was greatly enjoyed and a little later I descended for tea which was enormous. I well remember it - piles of hot-buttered toast and sandwiches!

Pat arrived during tea. She was looking very pretty and smart in her white nurse's uniform, although a shade thinner than when I had last seen her. She had lost those dark circles under the eyes. We sat together on a settee and had neither eyes nor ears for anyone else until we had heard each others' stories. Her operation was a minor affair necessitated because of morning sickness and occasional nausea. She thought that it occasioned an abortion but did not know, as she wasn't sure that she was 'enceinte'. She told me that she loved her work and had overcome her previous inability to stand the sight of blood. In fact, she was now able to carry out the operation of getting blood from a donor by herself.

Derek (Pat's brother) came in at 6 o'clock for a few minutes. He was a sergeant in a FMSVF transport unit and was able to slip away for an hour or two every now and then. He had been in Kuantan earlier in the campaign, but by now all Volunteer units were congregated in Singapore.

Elsie, Pat's sister, who had arrived with Pat, told me that Bill (her husband) was a liaison officer with 11th Division and might call in to Eden Hall at any time.

I asked Pat if she would like to dance at Raffles, which she agreed, so I rang to reserve tables for dinner and later in the dance hall. Freddie wanted to accompany us (rather tactlessly I thought, as Pat and I hadn't seen each other for a month). However, off we went about 8.30pm. Both Freddie and I were in uniform and carried revolvers in accordance with strict orders.

Raffles was crowded and it was no easy matter to get a table for cocktails. However a few words to Sarkies did the trick and we got quite a good table on the edge of the dance floor. About 70% of the men were in uniform - Navy, Army, Air force, Police, or Emergency Services. There was also a sprinkling of Dutch Officers.

Everyone appeared to be in the highest spirits. It was amazing that people could be so carefree when a battle for the country was raging less than 100 miles away. Bombs might demolish the whole building and everyone in it at any moment. However, the majority of the people in Raffles that night were Singapore residents to whom the war so far was only a name. They all thought that the enemy would be held and shortly driven back.

At the same time, it was all thoroughly enjoyable. It was pleasant to meet old acquaintances again. Drinks were quaffed with gusto and time passed quickly. Dinner was frugal, consisting of soup, fish or meat, vegetables, and sweets, and not particularly well-cooked. It was only because I knew the headwaiter that we were able to have cheese as well. Then, after dinner, we danced occasionally but it was much more interesting to watch and to have people coming up to one's table for a drink and a chat.

There was a strange air of unreality over the whole scene. Everyone was drinking and quite a number were not entirely sober. Conventionality was almost entirely lacking, and there was a lot of unrestrained loud laughter. It was, I thought, gregariousness in its worst form - the herd instinct at the first sign of danger. A sense of insecurity, so-far unacknowledged, urged people to eat drink and be merry. As yet, the probable sequel to it all went unrecognised. Facing the inevitable was avoided until the vaguely-felt danger had crystallised.

We went home before the dance ended and I slept without stirring until 9 o'clock.

CHAPTER 4

Withdrawal to Singapore Island

17th January

Pat had a free day, so we just had a lazy time. Freddie went off to see about his reinforcements and stayed out for tiffin.

There were no air-raid alarms during the day, but I inspected the shelter. It was above ground, quite spacious and well-constructed. Benches on either side were covered with cushions and rugs and it was lit by electricity. It could accommodate 20 people comfortably. The servants had similar one near their quarters, which I was told they would rush into pell-mell at the first suspicion of a warning, and would not emerge until the last note of all clear.

We had an early dinner and retired early.

18th January

Freddie set out before breakfast and returned to collect me at 10 o'clock. He had picked up 120 men at reinforcement camp, and sent them on ahead in four lorries.

Pat went off to work feeling happy that I was safe and knowing that it would probably not be long before I wangled another trip to Singapore.

We joined the convoy near Johore Bahru but had to stop for an air-raid warning and take cover. We saw 27 planes flying high over Singapore. AA guns blazed away at them but got nowhere close. The planes carried on their way and dropped their load on the Naval Base at their leisure, and clouds of smoke rose. None of our planes were in evidence.

<u>19th - 24th January</u>

Back at the Oil Palms Estate, the regiment concentrated on maintenance, gun drill, and small-arms practice on an improvised range on the estate. I attended several gun drills and got quite a lot of practical experience in artillery methods. I also read a lot of artillery manuals and studied notes made by Tony Willis when he had done his gunnery course in India. I took over the Survey Section, since I was now officially recognised as Regimental Survey Officer. I had the section out each morning for practice. Artillery Survey practice is standardised, and I found no difficulty adapting to Military methods.

A Punjabi Mussalman gunner was detailed as my orderly but he was the densest, laziest, sloppiest individual I have ever encountered. After a couple of days he was put on a charge of theft and awarded field punishment - so we didn't see much of each other. My next orderly was of the same race. He was not of sparkling intelligence, but he was OK. All the Regiment, apart from the 22 officers, were Indian although the Signal section included one European sergeant and two European NCO's. All the Indian officers, with one exception, were Viceroy Commissioned Officers (VCO's) whose ranks were Jemaldar, Jemaldar Major, Subadar, Subadar Major. They were excellent fellows to a man. They were not members of the officers' mess, but had their own messes. The exception was a charming Hindu officer who ranked as Lieutenant holding the King's Commission, having been promoted from VCO.

I felt it was essential I should learn Urdu, so with the aid of a small Urdu grammar and our doctor (a Hindu), it was not long before I could understand simple sentences and make my basic requirements understood.

A few antique planes, such as Buffaloes, Wildebeestes or Hawker-Horsley and some Dutch planes, were occasionally seen flying low, but there were swarms of Jap bombers on their way to or from Singapore, usually in formations of 27.

One afternoon, I drove to Niyor Estate where the British Batallion was resting. I was told that their kit had been sent on to Singapore, including my kitbag. This was most annoying, as I now lost hope of regaining my kit. However, whilst in Singapore, I had kitted myself from my cabin trunk and suitcases which had been sent down from Ipoh. I had also bought a new dressing case, camp bed, and a roomy tin trunk which I decided was the best way to keep my belongings.

25th January

The Regiment was ordered to go to Sedanak Estate, and as usual I was sent ahead with the recce party. We got there at 10 am and found good harbours for the Batteries. Our HQ was to be the estate manager's bungalow.

The estate manager was an old friend of mine, Fred Pierpoint, who had commanded the JVE prior to Jack Crosse. He gave us every assistance. There were other units already on the estate, including troops from 45 Brigade. They were an unkempt, unshaven, bedraggled lot - but no doubt they had endured every sort of privation. I didn't meet them myself, but I met General Heath, the Corps Commander, on his way to talk to them.

Whilst waiting for the Regiment to arrive, we accepted Pink's invitation to lunch at his modern, roomy bungalow. His house was in rather a muddle as his sister-in-law, Mrs Johnson, was leaving with a carload of suitcases, bound for Singapore. Her plan was to stay at Raffles until a berth in a ship sailing for Europe was available.

After lunch, Jack Crosse and Johnnie Johnson arrived. Jack was looking very fit but older than when I had last seen him - when he was best man at my wedding! He told me that the JVE were just up the road from Sedenak, and I promised to call in on him when I could.

Then orders arrived to look for a harbour near Skudai. It was difficult to find anything suitable there, but as it was getting dark, we decided to use rubber land on either side of a side road, even though the soil was fairly soft. We quickly allocated Battery areas and reserved an area for our HQ close to an office and factory.

Some Tamil labourers directed me to the manager's bungalow 100 yards away. It was a tumble-down old place. Inside was a woman and two officers, drinking with the manager. I recognised the woman - Alma Toby, previously Malayan ladies tennis champion. I was invited to join the party but when I explained my business it disturbed the civilians. The manager's main concern appeared to be his shipments of rubber and how they would be affected by war being so close by. Evidently no thought crossed his mind of evacuating his property to leave the military with a free hand, nor of getting his wife to safety.

When the Regiment finally arrived, we billeted ourselves in the Estate office and on the verandahs of adjoining buildings.

26th January

In the morning, Guy Cowie and I set out to reconnoitre the area. I had known it slightly in 1930, but time had changed it entirely, as it was now almost all under pineapples and rubber and criss-crossed by so many roads that a guide was desirable, unless one risked getting lost.

I suggested a visit to a nearby estate to meet Lloyd, the manager. He was half-Italian and used to be friendly with Lois *(my sister)*. His knowledge of local conditions and the vicinity proved invaluable to us. In fact, he was the only man who could have given us the information we needed. He took us around the whole area (about 50 or 60 square miles) in his car. He even took us to a Radio Location Station on a high hill overlooking the Straights of Johore. It seemed unusual for a civilian to have been given the entree to such a jealously-guarded spot.

The road to the Station was carefully camouflaged and was a masterpiece of engineering. It was fenced around with barbed wire and covered by machine guns. The guards were armed with tommy guns. There was a dummy road on the reverse side of the hill to deceive the enemy, although it was unlikely he would succeed in recognising the place as a Radio Location Station - because the buildings were well camouflaged and most of the machinery was underground.

The RAF personnel there were unfeignedly glad to see us. They said they felt unprotected and indeed they were extremely vulnerable, stuck away in the wilds, for they could not have offered much resistance. They told us that they were under orders to stand-by for a move to Java. Equipment such as theirs was too hush-hush, and too valuable, to be allowed to fall into enemy hands.

I warned Guy not to be too open with Lloyd, for although he was a member of the Volunteers and had given us invaluable aid, he was half-Italian.

After all this, we met up with the Battery commanders. Guy gave the location of his Battery HQ and allocated areas for which they would be responsible and asked them to submit their plans the next morning. The Signal officer was ordered to get to work immediately laying cables from each Battery to Regimental HQ. They were all laid before dinner. It was a heavy day and I was glad to turn in.

27th January

I accompanied Guy on an inspection of the Battery areas in the morning. In the afternoon I received leave to go to Singapore and lost no time getting there. I found Pat well and happy, but told her that I would feel happier if she went to Australia at the first opportunity. She only laughed at me - told me I was a defeatist etc. She quoted names of many other women who had not evacuated. I knew that argument was useless as the only real reason I could give for insisting that Pat should go was an intense conviction that Singapore would fall, which I could not put into words. As there appeared to be no immediate danger, I said nothing more on the subject.

Pat told me that the bombing had been frightful each day, but none had hit Tanglin so far. Everyone at Eden Hall was full of courage, especially Uncle Eze, who said he would never leave Singapore. Uncle Dick Gordon, who was frightfully British, said that Britain would never be defeated by these little yellow blanks and that any day now the tide would turn - we now had Spitfires who would knock hell out of the Japs and reinforcements were arriving each day, and so on. Anyway, it was grand to be among these delightful people again, to have real comfort and a sense of well-being, and above all, to have the charming ministrations and gentle thoughtfulness of my unparalleled wife heaped upon me.

Bill Hall was there, and Elsie was as happy as could be, in sure knowledge that her wonderful husband Bill was safe. We enjoyed our aperitifs before dinner on the verandah in the cool of the evening, and although we talked a lot about past present and tomorrow, none of us cared to think further ahead than that. The future, as a topic of conversation, was taboo, by mutual unspoken consent.

One of Uncle Eze's cars had been taken by the authorities, and today he had the other taken from him. It was only after representations by Bill that it was returned to him. Dick Gordon had his own car with a label on the windscreen with the magic words 'Not to be impressed' - but even this talisman did not save him, because the next day it was taken from its parking place, and he never saw it again. Dick's job was patrolling the main pipe-line from the Causeway to Bukit Timah.

Pat shared Elsie's little sports Morris - a beautiful little car which Elsie could not drive so that the car was virtually Pat's. Bill had his own car which he was in no danger of losing, being in the Police. He was very fed-up at not being able to get a job, either Police or Military, which would absorb his energies and I think the poor chap felt it rather keenly. Singapore was full of police from up country who had nothing much to do, as all the civilian special police had been called up to deal with the emergency work, and the supply of police exceeded demand.

I was told that Vivian [*Aunt Trilby's son from her first marriage*] had managed to get away occasionally from his military duties as one of a machine-gun crew in a pill box on the sea front. He always had a complete repertoire of hair-raising stories to recount. It was hard luck on Vivian. He had been on leave in Australia when war broke out, and he had raised heaven and earth to get a seat in a plane to Singapore. When he arrived he was promptly mobilised and subjected to stringent discipline - a form of constraint he had always found particularly irksome!

There was word from Mum and Aunt Trilby, saying that they had arrived safely in Perth, and an urgent request from Aunt Trilby to Eze asking for more money.

It was a cheerful evening and I revelled in the luxury of it all.

<u>28th January</u>

Pat and I were up early. Pat went to her Blood Transfusion Centre and I went back to Skudai, where I again accompanied Guy on inspection duties in the area.

Our duties were not clearly defined. However, we were forbidden to destroy boats without permission of the Harbour Master Johore Bahru. It was a stupid prohibition because the area was full of boats of all descriptions, both on the river and hidden in the mangrove.

The Manager and his wife had drinks with us after dinner, and they both got rather merry and vulgar. I didn't care for either of them. He could only think of his estate and the wrong-doing of the military in damaging his rubber trees and his property.

29th January

In the afternoon, Knox and I were ordered to go to Pontian and report our activities to 28 Brigade HQ. The journey was pleasant enough, and after the Skudai cross-roads, the road was fairly free of traffic. Darkness fell when we were about 15 miles from Pontian and we did not meet another vehicle thereafter. I was glad when we finally reached Pontian because we had been warned to look out for Jap snipers.

We found Brigade HQ near the hospital. The Gurkha sentries were very sensitive, and it was not easy to convince them that we were not Japs in disguise. I must admit that we had forgotten the password and I could only remember yesterday's - which was 'Dhobi'. The Brigadier was very pleasant and did not appear unduly worried. He gave us a whisky and soda. I told him what we were doing, with which he was quite satisfied, and we duly left. The drive home was uneventful but not pleasant. And so to bed.

30th January

Guy and I set out early to explore whether a particular track, 20 miles up the Pontian Road, was passable. We passed a large concrete device designed to stop tanks. It looked to me as though it was a sheer waste of time, since most of the land all around the barrier could be easily navigated by any tanks.

We found a Supply Depot at Choh, at the head of the Pulai River which is navigable by junks and small steamships. It contained several thousand tons of tinned food which Supply personnel were trying to salvage by lorries and junks, but not enough transport was available to send more than a few hundred tons per day to Singapore.

At the 20-mile point, we turned into a rubber estate, and came to a wooden bridge over a small stream, which had collapsed. Continuing on foot for half a mile, we came to a fairly large Chinese settlement, where the inhabitants fled incontinently at our approach - apparently taking us for Japs. I found an old Chinese in one of the Coolie lines who pointed us in the right direction, and after a few hundred yards we came to a prosperous-looking bungalow belonging to a Chinese Towkay. He gave us a cheerful reception, and after regaling us with ginger-pop, drove us in his car the remaining few miles to the village in the pineapple area.

In the afternoon we received orders for a general withdrawal into Singapore Island and for the Regiment to harbour in the Mandai Road. We were to leave as soon as possible after dark. As we were short of prismatic compasses, I drove into Johore Bahru and managed to procure about 15 quite satisfactory ones, as well as drawing paper, tracing paper, and various other odds and ends.

The Regiment moved at dusk, as ordered, and crossed the Causeway at 20.00 hours. We slept that night in the open, on a breezy hill-top near the Mandai Road. The fresh air was most enjoyable after our nights in the stuffy rubber factory.

31st January

After breakfast, I was sent to the Survey Office in Johore Bahru to search for maps. I picked up a number of coolie covers as well as maps, as the Regiment was very short of tents. Wilson took me to the new Survey Office in the palatial Government offices which contained a lot of stores. I was sorting out a heap of tents with Wilson when we suddenly heard the whistle of falling bombs, and then all hell seemed to break loose. The explosions seemed very close and I wondered whether the building would stand up to it. It was ten stories high and we were on the third floor.

At the first sound of bombs, we flung ourselves to the floor. When it was over, we rose to our feet, dusting ourselves, and remarked: "that lot was pretty close!" Actually, it was about 200 yards away. The place was full of smoke and dust. I heard later that bombs had fallen all around the Railway station, which was near Corps HQ. The bombing was obviously the result of 5th column work.

On my way back, I saw that the main Chinese store in Johore Bahru being looted by soldiery. Since we were about to evacuate Johore Bahru, I saw no reason why I should not join in. I stopped my truck and went to investigate. Lots of stuff still remained and I loaded up the truck with pickles, sauces, jams, soups, asparagus, raisins, cherries, potted meat, wines and cider until it could hold no more. It was a good haul, and the arrival of the truck back at HQ was hailed with acclaim since we were getting rather short of stores. A large proportion was handed over to the Indian officers and other ranks.

In the afternoon, I received permission to go to Singapore to enquire about my application for a Commission. When the Regiment was in Kluang I had called on JD Hall and given him a copy of my original application to the CO. He promised that he personally would see that it went direct to the Governor. I saw him again in Singapore, occupying a corner of a room in the Secretariat with Ivery, and he told me that he had handed my application to Pretty, the Under-Secretary, but that he had heard no further word - and with this I had to be content.

I went to Mount Sophia, where the Survey Department had temporary premises in part of a school, to try and get some survey data that we required. I talked to Husband, Cobon, and Bridges who told me they had been forced to leave KL in a hurry, and the department records were in a terrific mess - but of course this was the case for any large Department. Unfortunately, the data I wanted was not available, but they advised me to try the Adjutant of the Survey Company, whose HQ was nearby.

Bridges congratulated me on my commission. He was surprised when I told him that it was not yet finalised. He said that a paper from the SHC had come through to him the previous day asking him if he had any objection (in the usual way) and he had assumed the matter was now finalised. He advised me to put my pips up in the meanwhile, as it was possible I might hear nothing more about it for several weeks. Several officers of the Survey Company were in a similar position and were wearing their badges of rank in anticipation.

Eventually, I located the Survey Company. Himely was there, surrounded by piles of instruments and uniform. He was not able to supply the information I needed either, but he gave me some useful hints. He told me that his wife and children were in Australia.

I called in to Eden Hall. Pat had returned from the Blood Transfusion Centre and Olive was there too. They introduced me to some visitors - Mr and Mrs Smallwood and two of their relations. All residents of Johore Bahru had been evacuated the previous day, and the Smallwoods, with whom Olive had been staying, had taken up residence at Eden Hall. I gathered this was greatly to the annoyance of Elsie, but, appreciating that at a time like this everyone must do their best to help, she managed to conceal it. After dinner, I returned to our bivouac on the hill in Mandai Road and enjoyed a good sleep.

1st February

I heard a report that General Wavell and the Far East Command had gone to Java, and a little later heard the explosions which signalled the blowing-up of the Causeway between Malaya and Singapore. The batteries started to move into positions which had been reconnoitred the previous day, and HQ moved to a new harbour on the Thompson Road. The traffic stream along Mandai Road to Thompson Road was never-ending and it was hard to keep the convoy together.

En route, I was stopped by a strange officer who asked if I was armed and told me that parachutists had come down near the Garden Golf Club. I found out later that his information was false and he should have been dealt with as a fifth columnist. Fortunately I did not act on the information, but I told Guy later.

We found a first-rate harbour in an old Chinese storehouse which had lots of good cover. A Chinese pig-farmer had his hut nearby, and I managed to gain his goodwill and co-operation early on, by presenting him with some tinned food and by offering him money (which he refused) as rental for the building we occupied.

The rest of the day was taken up with arrangements for cooking places, latrines, bathing places, drinking water (which we secured by digging a well). As usual, slit trenches were dug everywhere. Guards were arranged, and the Signal Section busied themselves laying cable connecting us up to the Batteries and Brigade HQ (RA). The smell of the pigs got rather high on a hot day, but we got used to this.

2nd February

I spent the day attending to various duties. The bathing arrangements for officers and for other ranks were not very satisfactory, so I had a small stream dammed and we soon had a deep pool available. Some of the local inhabitants objected to the use of their wells by the Batteries and had to be pacified.

I reconnoitred the area about a mile around our harbour. I estimated there were about 100 civilians there - nearly all Chinese, apart from a few Tamils and Sikhs, but crowds were leaving Singapore daily hoping to find safety in the countryside.

All units had been warned to keep a lookout for parachutists and 5th Column activities of all kinds, and had been advised to take full precautions against a surprise attack by 5th Columnists.

All units were also advised to detail an officer to familiarise himself with the terrain in the neighbourhood of his unit's HQ and investigate the bona fides of all civilian residents in that area. I was given this responsibility, so I established friendly relations with the inmates of a number of huts in the vicinity. I noticed a derelict Hillman saloon car in the rubber, but in first rate condition apart from two punctured tyres. I was told that some soldiers had left it there the previous week. No clues as to ownership, but it was a 1940 model, registered in Singapore. On returning to HQ, I asked the Jamadar to see whether he could fix it.

Later in the afternoon, I asked Guy Cowie if he would like to have dinner at Eden Hall. Uncle Eze had given me carte blanche to invite any officers from the Regiment as guests at any time. Guy accepted, and we had a most pleasant evening. He enjoyed it all thoroughly and told me that he felt much better after this touch of home life. I think he had been feeling his responsibility very keenly lately.

3rd February

Guy inspected all the Batteries in the morning, and I accompanied him. We went first to 4 Battery, where I was able to help by inducing the owner of a Chinese house near the gun position to allow the Battery officers to occupy his home on payment of a weekly rent. Their two 6 inch Howitzers had been doing a little shooting and had hit the Johore Bahru Government buildings - which were suspected of being used as an OP. The OP for 4 Battery was behind a large rock on the face of the hill and had already been subjected to heavy shelling. Edward Sawyer was a bit of a wreck as a result of shells bursting nearby.

We next visited 21 Battery. They had done some firing during the night on the mouth of the Sindai River on which some movement been noticed. John Sopper, the commander, was very worried about 5th column activities. He said that the telephone cable from the OP was continually being cut and he personally had been sniped at, whilst on his way to and from the OP. Another officer had been shot at from close range whilst in the OP. He said the Naval Base was full of Asians who had no right to be there, and it was impossible to catch them in the maze of buildings. Also, he was very anxious about having to pull out quickly as the road out was visible from Johore in several places - even though a mat screen had been put up along the most exposed bit of road. Guy promised to put up his case to the CRA but didn't hold out much hope of getting him to change his mind as he was quite aware of the situation.

We passed through the Naval Base on our way to 7 and 10 Batteries. It was like a city of the dead, except for a few evacuating Military and Naval units. The railway line had rolling stock for miles. Some oil tanks were burning fiercely, sending up clouds of smoke (though nothing compared to the conflagration there would be a day or two later). The previous night, an enemy bomber had flown low over the Naval Base in the moonlight. At the time, we thought it was one of ours as it had all its navigation lights burning. However, a few seconds later, there were explosions, and several oil tanks were set ablaze.

Our drive through the Naval Base was indeed a sad one. This was a bulwark intended to defend British prestige in the East. It was a colossal work on which thousands of men had toiled daily and on which some of the best brains in the Empire had given of their best for more than ten years. It was now deserted and the habitation of skulking 5th Columnists.

7 and 10 Batteries were near Sembawang Aerodrome, which was still in use. I noticed many Spitfires parked under the rubber, many a long way from the aerodrome. Both batteries were well concealed, but being on flat land, the only fear was that their flashes might be visible at night. Guy had a few comments to make in this regard. They were all in tents, but also had the use of a few old Chinese huts. On the whole, they appeared to be very comfortably situated, with radios and plenty of food and creature comforts.

Back to HQ for lunch, after which I toured the area and found dozens of civilians, mainly Tamil, pouring in from Singapore. The local Chinese were renting out all available accommodation (even disused pigsties) to the newcomers. They were reaping a rich harvest, because for a shack 12 foot square they were asking the first month's rent in cash and $50 per month thereafter.

Lots of Sikhs had also filtered into the area. On questioning, I found that they were mainly police from the Naval Base who had been disbanded. I heard later there had been trouble on the Naval Base with the Police and many of them had simply deserted. However, they said they had been very unhappy about their treatment by the Naval Authorities and if they were offered employment as police or soldiers they would willingly accept.

One Chinese pig farmer told me that he had been thirty years in Malaya, ten of them as a building contractor, and was acquainted with numbers of Europeans who could vouch for him. He said that he suspected a group of Tamils, who occupied a house near him, could be 5th columnists.

He had no hard evidence, so I told him to pretend to take no notice, but to use his eyes and ears, and to ask any friends in the neighbourhood to do the same and report anything suspicious to me.

By this time, the LAD had done some small repairs to the derelict Hillman, and they reported that it was a first rate car. Guy agreed to my request to take it on the Regimental strength of transport, so I now had a good car at my disposal. Clearly it was useless to try to search for the owner.

Air activity increased. About 50 Hurricanes had arrived, but we heard that the pilots were unused to them, and as they were never sent up in formation they were dissipated away. All remaining bombers were sent to Sumatra when the withdrawal of forces to Singapore was completed. We were told they would continue their activities from Java, but we never saw them again. I heard Nee Soon village had been pattern-bombed and razed to the ground during the afternoon - not long after Guy and I had passed through.

<u>4th February</u>

I had a quiet night. After breakfast, I accompanied Guy on his Battery inspection, first to 4 Battery who had very little to report, and then to 21 Battery. We decided to approach 21 Battery over land from the Mandai Road. The map was quite accurate and we had no difficulty in making our way through rubber, undergrowth and swamp about 3 miles, almost direct. We thought it was better to go overland rather than risk the exposed spots along the Bukit Timah and Marsiling Roads unnecessarily. Also, we wanted to become acquainted with the country in case the Battery was cut off and we were forced to withdraw cross-country.

John Sopper was even more concerned about moving from his vulnerable position. He stressed that the infantry defence between him and the shore was very thin, apart from the Straits of Johore. He also reiterated the danger to the OP from 5th Columnists.

We inspected 7 and 10 Batteries but there was nothing untoward, and after a drink with the officers we returned to HQ, passing through (the razed) Nee Soon village. On the way, a large formation of enemy bombers flew overhead and pattern-bombed a target on the Naval Base - probably the oil installations again. Jap bombing was very accurate.

Colonel Hughes returned from Hospital in the afternoon, having recovered from all effects of his operation, and took command of the Regiment from Guy. This rather crowded the sleeping space available in the hut, so Dizzy Coleman and I moved into a tent nearby. Dizzy had returned to the Regiment after our withdrawal on to the Island, but he continued his long absences with Brigade and Divisional HQ. I rather think that he had some congenial companions there, as his liaison duties could not have been very arduous.

CHAPTER 5

Pat leaves Singapore

5th February

Once again, I inspected civilian activities in the area. More Tamils and Chinese had continued to pour into the area, but finding no accommodation, they erected their own huts - for which the Chinese landowners demanded exorbitant ground rent.

We received orders during the day to raise a detachment from the Regiment to man four 18 pounders on the South Coast. They were duly sent. We did not know under whose command they came, and never received any news about them again.

In the evening, I drove to Eden Hall with Tony Willis. We both enjoyed ourselves immensely and it was a great treat for Tony. Once again I suggested to Pat that she should take the first boat available to Australia - but with no result. She quoted Elsie and Bill to me. She said that if they had agreed that Elsie should stay on, even with two children in Australia, how much more was it her duty to stay on! I spoke to Elsie on the subject and found her foolishly adamant. However, when she told me that there were evacuation plans for all female hospital staff in case of emergency, I felt more reconciled to things. I knew it would break Pat's heart to have to leave me before the last possible minute.

6th February

I set off to Singapore in the morning to try and find out what was happening about about my commission. The air raid warning sounded as I was passing the Cricket Club, and I got out of my car and sheltered in a trench on the padang. When the all-clear sounded, I rose and found that Tungku Abu Bakar of Johore had been sheltering in the next trench. He was with Lanky whom I was glad to see again. Lanky told me that he had sent his wife and children away some time ago to NZ. He and Bu had apparently been bringing cattle from up-country and had managed to bring 600 from Johore. Bu told me that he would never kow-tow to the Japs -whatever his father did. Some days later, I heard that Bu had sailed for Australia with his family and was being given a Government pension of $5,000 per annum.

I found JD Hall and Ivery in the Treasury vaults where an office had been set up to conduct FME and VMS business. All the upstairs offices in the Secretariat and Treasury were quite deserted. Some of the offices had moved to the new Supreme Court. JD told me that nothing further had been heard of my commission and in the circumstances it was not surprising.

After this, I went to Wing Loong's to be measured for bush-shirts and shorts. We had an air-raid warning whilst there, but no-one bothered taking cover.

I had arranged to meet Pat at Raffles at midday. We had a few drinks and a poor lunch there. The band played selections as usual and the place was crowded. We met many people, including Norman Kennedy who was most amusing. He was in the Special Police and took it all as a huge joke. I also talked to Sid Smith and his wife Madge (nee Aubrey) whom I had not seen since we last met in London. They had no plans for the future.

After lunch, Pat returned to her work at the Hospital and I went on to John Little's and paid my bill. It was very disorganised there and the few staff on duty were quite insufficient to cope with the customers. One had to more-or-less serve oneself. Robinson's had received a hit from a bomb which had rather made a mess of the place, but they had tidied it up as far as possible and were carrying on their business as best they could. I visited the bank where Ritchie was in charge of the Alor Star section. At Pat's request he had cabled all my surplus cash except for about $1,200 to Australia (this $1,200 still stands to my credit with the Chartered Bank), and I drew some money for current expenses.

I returned to Eden Hall, where Auntie May and Olive gave me a good tea. Then, I had a hot bath and a change - after which I felt fine. I had a chat with Uncle Eze who was full of an optimism which it would have been a shame to disturb. He was very bucked at his foresight in stocking up with sufficient food and drink (mainly whisky) to see Eden Hall through for at least six months despite all possible calls on his hospitality - which were pretty high.

We had an air-raid during this time and it was wonderful how everyone had come to accept air-raids as part of the daily routine. So far, no bombs had been dropped closer than half a mile to Eden Hall. It was rumoured that shells had damaged homes in Stevens Road, but it was difficult to believe that the Japs had got guns capable of this long range.

I had dinner at Eden Hall and returned to Thompson Road, where I heard that the situation was more-or-less unchanged

- except that the Japs were now using observation balloons for spotting from the mainland. Light AA guns had successfully dealt with some of these.

7th February

I made a complete reconnaissance of our area in the morning and found little had changed. I warned the locals not to leave their residences unnecessarily. If too much movement was noticed they would be summarily confined to their houses.

I returned to HQ about midday and was asked by several officers if I had seen Major Cowie. I could not recollect having seen him after breakfast and thought that he had gone out in his car to visit one of the batteries. Then, at about one o'clock, one of the Sikhs reported that he had seen a British officer lying in the grass on the top of a nearby hill. My first thought was 'parachutist', and Dizzy and I hurriedly followed the Sikh about 200 yards to where he indicated a figure in the undergrowth. We approached cautiously, holding our revolvers at the ready, and it was not until we were within a couple of yards of the figure that we realised simultaneously that it was Guy. He was quite dead and had been so for some hours as rigor mortis had set in and flies were buzzing around him. There was a hole at the back of his head, and it was apparent that a bomb or shell-splinter had hit him. It was a terrific shock. It was the first time I had seen a corpse. Poor Guy! I said a short prayer for the repose of his soul and for his people.

His body was carefully carried down on a hurdle and sent off to the hospital with the MO. He returned a couple of hours later to say that Guy had been buried in the British Military Cemetery. We had thought that the Medical

Authorities would have given us at least two hours notice and we all regretted not attending the funeral.

I spent the rest of the afternoon making a list of his effects, after which I had his belongings packed up and sent to Divisional HQ for forwarding to his people. A letter arrived for him in the afternoon from a Miss Delano. I opened it, and after consulting Dizzy, replied informing her of his death.

<u>8th February</u>

On the 7.15 news, I heard with dismay and astonishment that the Japanese had landed on Singapore Island in the small hours of the morning, in force.

It really was a surprise, because the Governor, in his broadcast a few days earlier, had referred to our withdrawal to "Our Island Fortress". He sounded so confident that most of us thought that any effort by the Japs to land would be repelled - despite the apparent lack of fixed defences on the North of the Island. I had imagined that it would take at least two months for them to transport gear by rail or road in order to attempt a large-scale landing.

The enemy had landed in force (18 Battalions 1.5 divisions, I heard later) west of the Causeway, after a heavy bombardment. It seems that they suffered heavy casualties, but the Australians were caught unprepared. Their artillery apparently failed to respond to SOS signals and they were driven back.

I was told to set up MG posts on the perimeter of our area and to take particular care with regard to possible 5th Columnists in the neighbourhood. Guards were doubled.

There was a lot of shell-fire over our heads during the day, in addition to the enemy planes, and the noise of gunfire was fairly constant.

An old Chinese came to see me in the afternoon. He was very furtive and terrified that he might be seen speaking to me, so I took him into the hut. He told me that the previous night he had peered through a crack in the wall of a hut occupied by a lot of young Tamils and saw that they had revolvers and daggers. Since they spoke in Tamil, he could not understand what they were talking about. He had suspected these people for some days, as he had heard them expressing some very anti-British views to some Chinese. I thanked the old fellow for the information and drove to Divisional HQ. I recounted the story to the divisional Intelligence Officer who promised to send a Security Police officer to deal with the matter the next day.

We had no news of the Military situation. I hoped to hear that we had counter-attacked successfully, but the position remained obscure. Any rumours one did hear were generally most gloomy.

Tony Trench came to Rear HQ during the morning for something or other. He was exhausted and went to sleep while sitting down talking to me. I gathered that 4 Battery had had a strenuous time, having being fired at a good deal during the night. He told me that Dick Hare had behaved in a most gallant way, extinguishing a fire in a gun pit when its camouflage netting caught alight. Ammunition was stacked up in the pit and the situation was extremely dangerous, but Dick had carried on as if he was performing an everyday task. I heard later of similar incident in 10 Battery, where Terry was responsible for quick and decisive action in having a fire put out.

Incidents like these, which happen scores of time in action, inspire men with courage and faith in the leadership of their officers. It is only if they are witnessed by a CO (or similar officer) that official recognition of heroism is given - in the shape of an MC or similar award. In contrast, if an NCO was seen by an officer to have achieved the same task with the same efficiency, I don't think there is any doubt that the NCO would be recommended for an award immediately.

In the evening, I went to Eden Hall. During the journey I saw practical evidence of the shelling to which the residential area of Singapore was being subjected. I heard many shells whistling overhead and exploding a few seconds later, and also saw several houses which had sustained hits. The native population was beginning to show signs of alarm. Numbers of Asiatics were now returning to Singapore with every evidence of panic, whilst knots of natives forgathered on the roadside here and there, excitedly discussing the situation.

At Eden Hall, things were proceeding much as usual. There had been several air-raids during the day and several buildings near the hospital had been badly damaged. Civilian air-raid casualties were increasing. Pat told me that the blood bank was running very low, despite appeals daily to the public through the press. She admitted that she herself had given blood today. This was very noble of her because she could ill spare the blood after her recent operation, and in any case she dislikes operations or the sight of blood. I again pleaded with her on the subject we had so often discussed and told her how much happier I would feel if she were in Australia or South Africa, but it was impossible to move her - especially as she had the moral support of Elsie.

9th February

An officer from the Security Police called, and I discussed the Tamil 5th Columnists with him. We agreed that a posse of Military Police should come to RHQ soon after sundown and we would do a raid then - as they would be more likely to be at home at night than during the day. I spent the rest of the day on normal duties, interrupted by a good deal of shell-fire and bombing in the distance.

The Naval Base, which the Japs apparently suspected of being the source of hostilities, had been subjected to heavy bombing and shelling attacks. Most of the oil tanks were on fire and, every now and then, fresh tanks would catch alight. The smoke was like a heavy pall over the Island, and the sun shining through gave everything a most unreal appearance. There were other fires, mainly oil installations, but their combined effect was nothing compared to the Naval Base fire.

We heard there was fierce fighting in the north-west of the Island, and part of the Australian forces had been forced back to the main Johore-Singapore Road.

After dinner, a posse of 8 Military Police and an officer arrived. After arranging a plan of action, I led them to the Tamils' hut. It was pitch dark and we had about a mile to walk. We approached very cautiously and were not observed as far as we knew. Two men with Tommy guns were posted at each end of the hut, and two on either side of the door. The police officer opened the door quickly. We streamed in, all armed with revolvers. Our torches showed 20 men lying in their bedclothes on the floor. They were obviously amazed at our dramatic entry and put up no show of resistance. Lamps were lit, and the Tamils who were practically all English-speaking (late employees of the Naval Base) were herded into one end of the hut whilst a search was carried out for weapons or seditious papers.

After an extensive search of the hut and nearby ARP shelters, nothing incriminating was found. We carried on to another hut in the vicinity, also occupied by Tamil males, with a like result. I felt that the Tamils were innocent of subversive activities. The Chinese informant was either the victim of hallucinations as a result of spy-fever, or was attempting to work off spite against the Tamils.

Gunfire was heavy during the night, and the Naval Base fire (and many smaller fires at all points of the compass) lit up the whole sky.

10th February

Early in the morning, machine gun and rifle fire could be heard only a few miles off. I gathered from this that the situation had worsened. 4 Battery withdrew to a position in Nee Soon Cantonment facing north-west - confirming my view.

We were on the 'qui vive' in RHQ as there was always the possibility of attack by enemy patrols. I inspected MG posts, and made a thorough inspection of the area for any evidence of 5th column activities. Shells whistled overhead all day, and the crackle of MG and rifle fire was constant. Visitors brought alarming rumours of fighting near Alexandra Barracks and South of Bukit Timah - and still there was no talk of a counter-attack.

I decided to go to Singapore at the first opportunity and insist that Pat go by the first boat leaving Singapore, despite all her reassurances that arrangements were complete for the evacuation Hospital Staff when the situation demanded.

After lunch, we received orders to burn all confidential books and documents. It took Dizzy and I over two hours to comply.

At 5 o'clock, I received permission to go to Singapore for two hours. I fairly raced to Eden Hall. Pat had just returned from the Hospital and we were all together on the veranda. I decided to delay speaking to Pat until we were alone. I did not want to cause her or the others undue alarm. Frankly, whether the others stayed or not was their own concern, but it was imperative to me that Pat should go, and I did not want to indulge in further discussion on the subject. However, after a few minutes, Derek arrived on his motor-cycle, which he parked in the porch, and dashed up the steps in a state of obvious emotion. His first words were to the effect that Olive had to be prepared to leave on a ship sailing in a few hours for an unknown destination, possibly Australia. He told us that fighting was in progress at Alexandra, only a few miles away, and that the Japs might break through at any minute.

All was confusion immediately, but everyone reiterated their decision to stay. I took Pat to one side and insisted that she go with Olive. She agreed without further argument, and we went upstairs and packed quickly. Only three suitcases, because only a few personal belongings could be taken. I remember opening one of her suitcases at the last minute, and cramming in as many of her silver dressing-set as it would hold. I knew she would regret it if she didn't take them.

Elsie, with Bill's full approval, had decided not to go under any circumstances unless Bill was with her - so she said. Mrs Dickinson (wife of a GP) and Mrs Harris had decided to do likewise. So, unless they all changed their minds she must abide by their mutual agreement. It all sounded impractical reasoning - but no affair of mine.

It was a sad business parting from the girl who was more than wife to me. With every hour that I spent with her, she had become more and more firmly fixed in my mind as everything around which life revolved.

We had a long embrace before going downstairs to the car waiting in the porch. Olive was already in it, and her sister Margaret was at the wheel. The others were gathered around. We put Pat's luggage on board and the car left.

My final words to her had been to get aboard ship without questioning where the ship was bound or whether there was accommodation. Once aboard, she should allow no-one to put her ashore - short of physical force. I said the same thing to Olive.

Derek had gone before the girls drove off, because he had only a few minutes leave. I couldn't accompany them either, as I had only an hour's leave remaining, which I couldn't overstay under any circumstances. So, it was a blessing that Bill was able to go with them. He was in charge of traffic at the docks (which might have proved very useful). Shortly after they left, I returned to RHQ.

It was just a huge relief to me to know that Pat at least was on her way out of the inferno that Singapore promised to be. All I could hope for now was news that the ship had sailed safely with Pat aboard.

I had heard that the bombing of the docks in the last day or two had been intense and methodical. At least one ship bringing reinforcements had been sunk in the harbour. I gathered that labour at the docks was completely disorganised. Loading and unloading was spasmodically being done by troops. I prayed that the docks might be left alone during the night until the 'Gorgon' got away. However, since the enemy had not so far indulged in night-bombing on any large scale, there was every chance that she would get away.

Pat's passport was in order and she had a document in which the Malayan Government agreed to defray all transport expenses, authorising Pat to sail in any ship leaving Malaya. She had travellers' cheques and quite a lot of Malayan money. I had given her a bundle of papers which included my will and bank pass book. In the past few years I had invested a certain amount of money in Australia, through my solicitor. I knew he would disburse any money that she might require for expenses. Also, I knew that if I was killed, or taken prisoner if Singapore fell, that the Malayan Government would set up a representative in Australia. Any claims by dependants of government servants would be promptly and fairly dealt with. So, on the score of financial provision for Pat, I had no qualms.

February 11th

Smoke hung heavily overhead. There were many fires, including one on the enormous oil installation on Pulan Samboe. One began to have a feeling of impending doom. Guns had been firing all night and machine guns began to add their crackle to the general noise at dawn. Some sounded very near. Fortunately, our hide had managed to remain undiscovered from the air, escaping blitzes from shelling and bombing, although specimens of both fell nearby.

I did odd jobs in the morning, such as sorting out and cleaning survey instruments and inspecting MG posts. At mid-day, word came through that the RHQ was to withdraw about one and a half miles to rendezvous with 4 Battery.

It appeared that the Japanese had attacked on the left flank of 11 Division down the Mandai Road. Despite a concentration of gunfire on a height overlooking the Causeway, the ground could not be held and Japanese reinforcements came over the Causeway.

A Battery of Australian Field Artillery tried to harbour in our hide at Rear HQ in the afternoon. I managed to convince them that they would only disorganise our vehicle lines, so they pulled into the rubber alongside. They were in great disorder having had to withdraw in a hurry, and it took them a couple of hours to adjust themselves sufficiently to continue their withdrawal.

I went out with the Doctor to scour the countryside for medical supplies. Whilst doing so, I called in at Eden Hall and found them in a very nervous condition. My advice was to move to Raffles Hotel immediately. The Nassim Road area was so isolated that there was danger of enemy troops filtering through and the possibility of action in the Eden Hall vicinity. There was also going to be shell-fire, because our guns were in positions all around.

The rest of the afternoon was taken up with preparations to move. As soon as it was dark, the convoy moved off, but the traffic on the road was enormous, and it was impossible to keep together. Dizzy had gone to the head of the column as he had already recce'd the hide in the afternoon while I was out, and the Doctor and I brought up the rear of HQ B Echelon. It took two hours before we reached our destination, and another three hours before every vehicle was parked.

The night was pitch dark and, to make matters worse, a Field Ambulance Company nearby moved out at 2 am along the track on which a number of our vehicles were parked. I slept the night in the car.

<u>12th February</u>

I was up at dawn for a general rearrangement of vehicles to enable a swift withdrawal if necessary.

There was a deserted supply dump nearby, with no one guarding it. It included a hut crammed with cases of milk, rum, jam, chocolate etc, and we took several cases. There were also thousands of tins of petrol and kerosene, and we helped ourselves liberally to these - despite an order received that morning that no petrol was to be taken or destroyed without proper authority. There is no doubt that this dump, like dozens of others, subsequently fell into the hands of the enemy.

Many shells fell nearby and a battery not far away fired in reply for most of the day. Machine gun and rifle fire seemed to be extremely close. Of course, one of the first duties of the day had been to see that sufficient slit trenches were dug and machine gun posts established around the wagon lines, but even so we were extremely vulnerable. It was with relief that we welcomed the Colonel and Adjutant when they arrived shortly after 21 Battery.

The Colonel brought us up to date with the military situation, telling us that all British forces were going to withdraw inside an area around Singapore. This all sounded very depressing, because casualties in such a restricted area would be enormous. Every shell or bomb would cause loss of life. This was my first reaction (and I think everyone else's). However, we had a fine force of fighting men who were rapidly gaining war experience. We thought that a well-planned and executed counter-attack, after a few days in which to consolidate and reorganise, would drive the Japs back and initiate a forceful and determined counter-offensive.

Water was of prime importance, but I was told that the McRitchie reservoir, which we had to defend at all costs, held enough water for Singapore's needs for months. In any case, water could be obtained anywhere on the Island by digging wells a few feet deep, and rain could be relied on for at least a few days each month.

Even though there would be casualties, the risk of death and the chance of victory was far preferable to the certainty of being taken prisoner and subjected to the nameless tortures and shameful indignities that the yellow dwarfs would undoubtedly inflict on anyone sufficiently unfortunate to be captured.

It was common knowledge that the Japs would take no prisoners. So, the chances of death, one way or another, seemed fairly certain. We just had to make a last desperate effort to hurl the invader back and hold this last defensive position until relief arrived.

These were my thoughts as I considered the situation, and I think it reflected everyone else's unvoiced ideas, generally speaking. Any thought that our enemies might win the final victory were pushed into the inmost recesses of one's mind. The unexpressed (possibly repressed) fear of being considered a defeatist made it a possibility that was never consciously contemplated.

At about 3 pm, the Colonel and I set off in his car for Singapore via Yio Chu Kang Road, followed by one despatch rider. We went to the Police Depot in Thompson Road where we were unable to locate Div HQ. However, we found out that it was going to be established in Chancery Lane.

The road had been crowded with vehicles mainly proceeding towards Singapore. In general, the impression was that things were in a state of disintegration. Overturned lorries were common sights, as were cars and lorries abandoned for no apparent reason. We passed several military camps, all deserted and showing signs of having been left in a hurry. Dozens of tents were standing. The occupants had clearly not believed they had time to take them down, because they would have been a sought-after commodity if we had heavy rain in the next few days.

Military units occupied all houses in and around Chancery Lane. Div HQ was in Alsagoff's house. The CRA had his HQ in a small house at the end of a lane behind Div HQ. The whole of the area was well covered by trees which sheltered any activity from air observation. Precautions were always taken to park vehicles under cover and to refrain from movement during an air raid as far as possible.

The Colonel eventually received his orders about harbouring and gun positions. We were to harbour in the Newton Road area. We found that most of the houses which had good cover for vehicles, were already bespoken. The Colonel and I had several arguments with other officers before we found suitable quarters and cover.

Regimental HQ was established in a modern fairly large two-storied house in Newton road, and in its compound there was sufficient cover for about 12 vehicles. The Regiment was partly housed in the compound of an old bungalow-type house at the Circus end of Newton Road. The rest was in the compounds of small houses in lanes off and in the rear of Newton Road on the seaward side. The Battery commanders went off in search of gun positions soon after we arrived. Such positions were difficult to find, as guns were in action everywhere.

The lanes were very narrow and it was no easy task manoeuvring heavy vehicles and guns, but things were fairly well in order shortly after dark. The house in which been RHQ had been established was still occupied by its Chinese owner and his family. He had no objections to billeting us. On the contrary, he welcomed us, as he was glad of our protection. He threw open all the ground floor of his house, and gave us the use of his kitchen, so we were soon able to enjoy a really good meal and sleep - our beds being made up in the sitting room.

<u>13th February</u>

During the night, a number of shells whistled overhead and exploded unpleasantly close - shells from the enemy and, maybe, from us. It was clear we had a battery maybe a mile to our rear. The enemy and ourselves were exchanging compliments.

Slit trenches had to be dug early next morning and other normal routines carried out. After breakfast, I drove around to Eden Hall to see how Uncle Eze and family were faring. The house was shut up, all the blinds were down and the front gate bolted, so I decided to go and enquire at Goodwood Park Hotel, but it was completely deserted, although I found some troops billeted in the flat in which Mum used to live. No servants were to be seen. I was about to leave when a man suddenly emerged from a bedroom. It transpired he was the manager. He told me that Uncle Eze was now living at Raffles. The poor man was in a dreadful state. He was a foreigner of some description, and hadn't shaved for days.

Anyway, I wanted some shoes, so he showed me the room of a guest who had not occupied his room for days. There I found a decent pair of shoes - which I confiscated - only to find out later that they were too large for me. I gave them to the Colonel instead. I was not able to carry on to Raffles as there was something wrong with my car.

It was all quiet back at RHQ - apart from considerable shell fire. I asked Murray from 21 Battery if he would lend me his car. He agreed and said he would accompany me, but hearing of my visit to Goodwood Park, would not be satisfied until we returned and ransacked the place for drinks.

In the morning, an order had come that all stocks of spirits had to be destroyed to prevent them from falling into the hands of the Japanese. It was considered that if Singapore fell they might celebrate their victory, and under the influence of liquor might commit all sorts of atrocities. The manager informed me that this order had already been carried out at Goodwood Park, but a search of the cellars revealed any amount of rare liqueurs and wines - a quantity of which we took, together with some perishable foodstuffs, such as cheese and cold ham.

After this, we carried on to Raffles Hotel via Orchard Road. There were shell holes everywhere in the streets, and electric light and telephone wires were lying all over the place. Many houses and shop premises had been damaged by bombs or shells, and glass and debris was strewn inches, and, in some places, feet deep.

I saw something which I had first seen a few days ago - bands of troops roaming the street at their own sweet will. They were European and native, but Australians were pre-eminent. I heard later that Australian ancillary troops had been a perfect disgrace. There had been little, if any, discipline amongst them for some days and many of them had left Malaya without permission - in many cases boarding ships which were full of women and children and civilians, and refusing to be put off.

A story was told of a party of Australian soldiers at the docks who took possession of a launch intended for last minute evacuation of certain civilians. Against the wishes of the skipper and crew, they forced the launch to sail and the launch had to be fired on before they would return.

The road outside Raffles was lined with dozens of cars, military and civilian. The open spaces nearby were occupied by guns, although I saw none of them in action. Inside Raffles, it was a shambles. There were no servants to be seen, but occasional groups of people were sitting at tables -

on some of which were glasses and bottles of whisky or gin. There was debris lying all over the floor, and, as the place was in semi-darkness, the whole atmosphere was most depressing.

I located Aratoon Sarkees in the office. He told me that Uncle Eze had a room in the wing nearest the Raffles Institute on the ground floor. There I found Auntie May, Uncle Eze, and Dick all in the same room. Accommodation in that part of the building, which was of reinforced concrete, was at a premium.

If the situation had not been so pathetic it would have been amusing. Uncle Eze had had an indoor ARP shelter constructed by Gammons. In shape and size, it was somewhat like a large, very stoutly built, dog-kennel. When Murray and I entered the room, Auntie May opened the door. Uncle Dick was seated at a table and Uncle Eze was sitting in his ARP shelter. I understood that he spent most of his day there and slept in it at nights - emerging only for meals.

They were very pleased to see us and I was relieved to see that they were safe. We each had a glass of beer (I think there was a refrigerator in the bedroom). They had large stocks of tinned food and ample quantities of drink. Auntie May told me that the place had ceased to function as a hotel. The servants had all disappeared, and if one wanted cooked food one had to cook it oneself.

The kitchen had received a direct hit from a bomb some days before and was full of unwashed kitchen and eating utensils, most of which contained partly eaten food. Some of the women had attempted to wash up dishes and tidy things up. It was apparently an impossible task as other people kept on using the utensils without attempting to wash them up after use and generally the place was in a filthy and insanitary condition.

I asked them what their future intentions were and advised them to leave Singapore immediately - by tongkang or some other vessel. They said they would not leave under any circumstances as their future was wrapped up in Malaya. If Singapore fell they were prepared to take the consequences. They were all old people and not prepared to start new lives in another country. This was what they said to me, but I gathered that these objections really applied to Uncle Eze. Aunt May and Dick were bound by their word to Aunt Trilby [*now in Australia!*] - that in no circumstances would they desert Uncle Eze.

When we left Raffles there was an air-raid and bombs falling not far away. The streets behind Raffles were in a state of chaos - especially Middle Road. Dozens of shops had been flattened. Bomb and shell-craters pitted the road and progress was slow. Bukit Timah Road near Newton Circus was impassable. There was a huge bomb-crater right across the street and telephone and electric wires were tangled in confusion. Debris from bombed houses overflowed over the footpaths on to the roads.

We returned to Thompson Road via a detour. It had been pattern-bombed in our absence. Buildings had been damaged and there were severe casualties to native civilians (mainly servants). A number of our men were killed too.

One bomb had fallen on a lorry which had caught fire and set alight to another lorry alongside. Four or five men were killed in this explosion and several injured. Another bomb had fallen on the kitchen of a house next door to RHQ and killed several of our men and injured others who were in and around the kitchen.

The Colonel and RHQ moved out during the morning to join 53 Brigade HQ in Balestier Road, coming under the command of CRA 18 Div. This left me in complete charge of 4 Batteries B Echelon, with the exception of Murray who was in charge of his Battery down the road near Newton circus.

The Chinese owner of the house and his family decided during the morning that the locality was unsafe, and moved out in great haste. I promised them that their property would be respected and that no one would be allowed upstairs.

Nehtu (the doctor) and I had a good lunch, in the middle of which a shell exploded alongside the house but did no harm. After this, shell-fire increased alarmingly and, as the afternoon wore on, desultory rifle and tommy-gun fire not far away increased in volume - until at times I fully expected the enemy to appear. Air-raids were frequent and it became increasingly difficult to keep the men out of the slit trenches which they had so enlarged that they were practically ARP shelters.

There was one ARP shelter nearby in the grounds that could hold about 25 people, but it seemed to be permanently occupied by native civilians - servants from the neighbourhood and their families. However, fortunately, they departed before nightfall and I was glad to see them go, as it left the shelter free for us.

A large proportion of the rifle fire seemed to be not more than a hundred yards away. I decided to post a Lewis gun on the bank of the ditch in Newton Road in order to have a field of fire along the road. There were two men to each Lewis gun and two riflemen deployed either side of a gateway.

The firing became so intense and so close that lorries would halt for a while, judging it dangerous to proceed further. The drivers and passengers would hurriedly jump down and take cover behind walls or in ditches. I do not know to this day (and nor does anyone else) whether the firing was due to our men, firing nervously at imaginary enemies. Later. it was alleged that 5th Columnists (or disguised Japs) had been aimlessly firing guns – in an attempt to persuade everyone to believe that Japs had filtered through the front lines.

At any rate, there is no doubt it produced an incredible atmosphere bordering on panic. Although I did not actually witness any instances of cowardice, there is no doubt that men withdrew without orders under similar conditions in other parts of the Island. From what I heard, the Newton Road neighbourhood was unparalleled for the intensity and duration of this harmless, but ominously-forbidding, rifle fire.

Murray and I scoured the vicinity as stealthily and thoroughly as possible - revolvers in hand. We tried to locate the source of even one shot - as some of the shots sounded only a few yards away at times. However, the area was so closely built with large and small houses that walls, fences, and thick hedges made the place a complete maze. To reach a particular spot on the other side of a wall could entail quite ten minutes of careful stalking.

We questioned and searched every civilian we found. We ascertained the bona fides of all troops. We searched servants' quarters and ARP shelters. We looked up trees and made sure no 5th columnist was in the branches. However, all our efforts, aided at times by stray officers who happened to be passing down Newton Road, were fruitless. By the time we had finished, the firing close at hand had practically ceased.

From then on, I was kept busy making night arrangements with the Subadar-Major. I had a drink with Murray, who had found several infantry officers to join him in a most convivial night at his billet, and returned at dark to my quarters. The Doctor and I then had dinner.

The Doctor decided to sleep in the civilian ARP shelter with some of the Indian Officers, but I elected to sleep under the porch in the front of the house, rather than face the stuffiness and stench of the shelter. I also thought it would be more convenient if there was a night alarm.

No sooner had I gone to bed and dropped into a heavy sleep, than a despatch rider arrived with orders for me to report to the Colonel immediately. It was pitch dark and it took me a long time to find the HQ. I had to explore several lanes off Balister road and was challenged by numerous sentries.

The place was littered with men asleep on the floor. I found the Colonel and Adjutant in a small room. The Colonel told me to go to 7, 10, and 21 Batteries immediately, and collect the three toughest and most reliable men from each. I was to take them to Div HQ no later than 11pm, when further instructions would be issued. It was then 9.45 and I had only a vague notion as to where the batteries were, so it was no easy task. I was told that the party was probably going to form part of a commando. One European officer would be required to take charge of our draft - either Murray or myself. The easiest solution was to go myself, but as I was unfamiliar with Urdu I decided I should let Murray go.

At the first Battery, I hurriedly explained requirements and had great difficulty in getting the Battery Commander to understand the urgency. It took me15 minutes. I had a similar problem with the other Batteries. However, after much sweating and swearing, I managed at last to get them into a lorry and we sped to Newton Road. There, I dug Murray out of a sound sleep. He found it difficult to comprehend what was going on. The others were summoned in like fashion, and in a few minutes we were off to Chancery Lane, where we arrived at 11 pm precisely. We found a line of lorries full of silent men drawn up along the kerb. There was no light. Nanda (Staff Captain RA) loomed up and asked me if my party was complete, and I replied that it was. With that, he told Murray, who was beside the driver in the front seat, to take his place in the procession and it moved off a few minutes later.

I heard later that they were destined for evacuation. They embarked on warships and sailed that night. Some of the party probably got through. Others were torpedoed. As for Murray, he was heard of in Padang Sumatra, and presumably got to India - but no doubt had many thrilling adventures before he fetched up there.

With a sense of relief, I drove back to Newton Road and resumed my bed in the porch - only to be woken a short while later by the sound of shells whistling overhead and bursting not far away. In addition to gunfire, the sound of mortars firing their shells could be heard - and the sizz-z-z as they sailed overhead.

I began to think that the situation was getting dangerous when a shell hit the wall of the home with an ear-splitting explosion. This forced me to get up and to see if anyone was hurt. I had not been out of my bed for more than a few seconds when another missile hit the front of the house with a crash, bringing masonry tumbling down over the bed that I had been sleeping on.

For about an hour after that, shell and mortar fire was heavy. Many burst unpleasantly close. There was rifle and tommy-gun fire, not only to the North but all around us. After consulting the Subadar-Major, I decided to post guards all around the compound. Mortar fire was now coming from our rear and the Subadar-Major was convinced that the enemy had mortars mounted on lorries travelling the streets at will. This may have been the case, because, as far as I know, traffic on the streets was not interfered with. If Japs had been dressed as British troops and fired mortars from lorries on our side of the front line, no one would think it his business to question them.

It was a frightful night and I had no sleep at all.

CHAPTER 6

Surrender

14th February 1942

The bombardment died down as dawn approached. The small arms fire also grew more desultory, and shortly after dawn it ceased altogether. The house had received five hits during the night. The inside of the house and lawn was covered with debris, which I ordered to be cleared up as much as possible.

At about 9 o'clock, and hourly thereafter, the neighbourhood was pattern-bombed. Shelling and mortaring also recommenced. There was no damage, until midday, when a shell went through the front of the house and exploded in the open space between the house and the kitchen. This seemed to be the signal for a general barrage and the house received several more direct hits.

I had a terrific job trying to get the native troops out of their slit trenches and shelters. I knew it was dangerous for them to be out of cover during shelling and mortaring - but war is a dangerous business after all! At the time I thought the enemy would have had ample hiding-places in deserted buildings and innumerable ARP shelters, and might descend on us at any time. It was our duty to hinder them with all the measures in our power.

The Doctor was in a terrific state of funk and would not emerge from his ARP shelter for any reason, even though I often wanted him to interpret for me.

The previous night, the Colonel had said I could move B Echelons to any other locality I considered safer. I couldn't reconnoitre whilst the flap was on, but at about 3 pm Athol Long appeared and we went off on a tour which included the area between the Kallang Canal, Noulmein Road and Lavender Street.

The damage done in the built-up areas was incredible. Whole rows of houses had been flattened by bombs. Many roads were completely blocked by debris or bomb and shell craters. As for the New World, it had been gutted by fire the day before and was still smoking (I understand it had been a Supply Ammunition Depot).

Whilst on foot near the New World we saw a large formation of enemy bombers about to fly overhead. We took refuge in a shelter which we shared with a gun crew belonging to a battery in action nearby. After the planes dropped their bombs we emerged and returned to our truck. We found that a bomb had dropped about 50 yards away. There was no damage apart from a crater about 15 yards in diameter - but the truck was covered in red earth.

We eventually decided that a piece of land near a Hindu temple, about 200 yards towards Singapore from Serangoon Road Police Station, would be preferable to our present harbour in Newton Road - even though the locality was thick with guns and a target to the enemy. However, we could not be more of a target than we had been during the last 48 hours!

We returned to Newton Road about 5 pm and gave orders to prepare to move in 30 minutes. In fact, it took an hour and a half before the cortege was ready to move off. No vehicle could be left behind as none of the drivers knew our destination. That hour or so of preparation was full of hard work and worry. Several nervous drivers bogged their lorries and had to be towed out. There were several collisions. Many drivers and other troops had to be routed out of ARP shelters and dugouts - a task which took a lot of time. We found many of the troops were missing – deserted - although a few may have intended to come back.

By the time we got to our new harbour it was practically dark, but the job of parking went smoothly and efficiently. There was ample cover, with a grove of fruit trees near the Temple and some large Angenna trees. This was extraordinary as we were practically in the heart of Singapore. Whilst in transit the shelling had died down, but on arrival it recommenced. This served to ginger up the work of preparation of slit trenches. Fortunately, there were a number of shelters already constructed by former occupants and by nearby civilian residents.

Some Coast Defence gunners occupied one building, waiting only for dark before going into the front line as infantry. They were in a space under a small bungalow, only about 3 feet high, but bricked around and comfortably fitted with mattresses and blankets. We decided this should be the Doctor's RAP.

There was a natural trench about 30 feet long alongside a Buddhist temple. There was also a shelter about 4' 6" high and 4' square which gave one a fine sense of security, as a fence and an earth bank provided good protection.

The Subadar-Major was instructed where guards must be posted. After a hearty meal from tins and a bottle of beer, it was with relief that one could sink into oblivion without any danger of a surprise attack.

The barrage grew in intensity. Although I settled down to sleep, I was woken many times by the crash of shells exploding only a few yards away. I went back to sleep on each occasion, praying to God that a shell would not burst close enough to do us bodily harm. There were dozens of guns within a few hundred yards adding their noise to the general bedlam. Several fires started.

Physical exhaustion had put me beyond all thoughts of fear, but the Doctor was in a bad state. He annoyed me greatly during the night by trying to get closer to me - with the result that I had to speak firmly to him and ask him to keep to his part of the trench as there was insufficient room for two people to be side by side.

15th February

None of the troops were injured during the night - mainly because the ones who weren't on guard duty were well dug in. The ground was littered with leaves blasted from the trees. Many branches, large and small, were lying here and there. Pieces of shell-splinters were scattered around in profusion and it was obvious that we had been lucky.

It was a fine day, and one of the first things to attend to was the rough-messing arrangements for Athol, the Doctor and myself on the small verandah of a very small bungalow. The bungalow was locked, but there was no necessity to break in as the kitchen was open. More slit trenches had to be dug and dug-outs constructed. Vehicles had to be properly parked and camouflaged.

Shell-fire continued at intervals during the morning. Sometimes, shells burst very close and did a lot of damage to the shops all around. The sky was full of enemy planes all day and the 'crump' of bombs was commonplace. One only took cover when planes were about to fly directly overhead. A few troops were injured by shell-splinters during the morning, but none seriously. Actually, this surprised me, for most of them could only be induced to get out of the shelters with the greatest difficulty. Most of the shelters were old and contained water, but this did not abate the troops' passion for safety at any price!

There was a rumour yesterday that American reinforcements had landed in Penang and were pressing southwards to relieve Singapore. This gained credibility by force of repetition. Most of us hoped that if we could hold out for a few days Singapore would be relieved.

At about 11 o'clock, an order came from RHQ to collect and store all the ammunition available from a dump in Serangoon road. We set parties to work digging pits. We estimated 1200 rounds might be available. Six lorries were required, of which four were to be supplied by the batteries and two by B Echelon. The plan was to collect the ammunition at 1 o'clock.

Whilst the pits were being dug, I inspected some of the ARP shelters in the vicinity to see if any of our troops were sheltering in them. They had been forbidden to leave the compound in which we were camped. Sure enough, there were numbers of them - all of whom received a wigging from me (through the SM who accompanied me) and reluctantly and sheepishly returned to our wagon lines.

I met a gunner from one of the British Batteries nearby who told me that there had been constant sniping yesterday from the upper windows of shops and houses in the neighbourhood. He also told me about the devices for signalling to aeroplanes and, possibly, to the observation balloons which could be seen a few miles away. The favourite method was mirrors, so he said. Small mirrors, fixed or manipulated outside, or large dressing table mirrors inside a room and visible from outside. We walked down several back lanes, but I could see none of the methods he had described to me in use. He then pointed to a particular house and said that he was quite sure that there had been signalling from it yesterday - opening and closing windows - and he was also reasonably sure there had been some sniping. I decided to search the place and see if any evidence existed of signalling or sniping, or any other 5th Column activity.

The occupants, Chinese on the ground floor and Tamils on the other two floors, opened the front door with considerable reluctance. We searched the place quickly but found nothing of any interest, except that in a back room I found an army uniform and web equipment together with a pay-book that belonged to an Indian Private in the RASC. It was obviously a deserter who had decided that life as a civilian was preferable to army life. I kept the pay-book, intending to hand it over to the Military Police later with a report.

I returned to our lines. Whilst passing the Buddhist temple it crossed my mind that as Japs were Buddhists it was possible that the Temple might be a centre of 5th Column activity. Suiting action to the thought, I rapped on the back entrance to the Temple. I was let in without argument. In the rear quarters, there were about forty males and several females. It appeared they were all Siamese and nearly all had recently been released from the Civil Prison. One of them, who spoke English well, told me that he had been a school-master in Penang until he was arrested at the outbreak of war. He and several others looked very Japanese in appearance, so I decided to search them for firearms, but found nothing. We then searched the Temple - with the same result.

During the search, we decided to search inside the image of Lord Buddha. This was Lord Buddha seated cross-legged with on hand on his knee and the other raised in benediction. It was about 30 feet high and had a secret recess in the rear. However, the chamber was small and contained nothing but an altar and a few oddments of religious significance.

By 1 pm, the lorries were ready to collect the ammunition, apart from two which were to be picked up en route from 10 Battery. Athol had gone on to 10 Battery position during my absence, to hear their news and have a general yarn. There I found him, about to have lunch. Having never collected ammunition before and being unaware of the niceties of loading, I fully expected that Athol would see to it himself. He realised the drift of my remarks when I asked questions as to how many rounds could be loaded on to a 5 ton lorry etc. He said that there was no need for us both to do it, and he would go if I didn't want to. I certainly was not keen to collect ammunition. It seemed to me to be exceedingly dangerous. However, it was clear that he did not wish to accompany the party, so I made light of it and carried on.

The convoy consisted of myself, driver and escort in my car in the lead, and six lorries, each carrying a driver and two others. We drove up Serangoon Road, where there was practically no traffic, to the Braddell Road junction where there were three officers. They gave me directions to the ammunition dump, near an old house about 300 yards away. I was warned to be careful as the front line was just over the crest of a hill.

I found the dump without difficulty. It contained all kinds of ammunition. Only one lorry at a time could be loaded. All the 3.7 ammunition was in one spot. At first, there appeared to be no one in charge but then two Ordnance Sergeants appeared. They admitted they were nervous. They told me that in over the last 24 hours the rest of the dump personnel had deemed it advisable to disappear. This did not cheer me at all - especially as enemy planes flew overhead now and then, but I realised that one had to be fatalistic. I carried on loading as calmly as possible. Two or three lorries didn't load fully and although it was a temptation to let them go, I had to bring them back. The job took about an hour and it was with some relief that we left.

On the way back, I heard shouting in the Serangoon Road and stopped to investigate. Hundreds of Tamils, Chinese, and other natives - men, women, and children - were running down the road towards the city as hard as they could - thinking that the Japs had broken through.

I looked up the road behind the seething mob and could see nothing - apart from many overturned lorries and cars. Asking one individual as he ran past what the excitement was all about, he said breathlessly: 'aeroplanes, bombs!', and continued his blind flight.

A few seconds later, a formation of bombers pattern-bombed the area towards which the panic-stricken crowd was running. Immediately they turned about and ran in the direction from which they had come.

The drive back to HQ was uneventful. I had a bottle or two of beer with a belated lunch, when a chit arrived that a

'Cease Fire' would be ordered at 4 pm. It was incredible! Shameful! Surely we were not going to surrender?

It was unthinkable that our leaders were about to let us down like this! After all, the majority of troops had not come to grips with the enemy so far. I think that most of us had decided that hand-to-hand fighting was inevitable ultimately, and our fate would rest on the result. But to calmly consign us to humiliating captivity without even the chance of fighting for liberty seemed the basest of acts. So ran my reflections on receipt of the news - which had come as a bolt from the blue.

The fact was that we all (most of us anyway) had got into the habit of living in the present and suppressing any inclination to think of the future. Personally, my first reaction was to consider the possibility of escape.

After lunch, at about 3.30, I summoned the Indian officers and told them of the 'Cease Fire' order. They received the news without demonstration of joy or sorrow, but a general slackening in tension was obvious. This was exemplified a short while later, when the firing died down at 4 o'clock, by lively spirits and noisy chatter.

The Adjutant arrived and told us that most of our guns had been destroyed. Strict orders had been issued against any attempts to escape as the Capitulation was not to come into effect until 9 am tomorrow morning when the Japs would formally enter Singapore. In the meantime an Armistice existed. He told us that orders would be given later, as to how when and where the surrender of the Regiment was to be effected. In the meantime we were to stay where we were.

By 5 o'clock, only occasional gunfire could be heard - apparently from batteries who had not received the order or who neglected it. When I was crossing Serangoon Road, I was hailed by two NCO's of the Manchesters. They said they had been sent by their CO to get definite proof that the cease fire order was not the work of 5th Columnists, as they had received it third hand. Their Colonel was convinced that the order was bogus and was determined to fight on, regardless of what other units were doing, until he received definite proof. I could not reassure them and advised them to go to Malaya Command and obtain a written order there. Later on, I found out that the Manchesters, and indeed a number of other units, continued fighting until early the next morning.

After I crossed Serangoon road, I went to see what a British Battery near the New World was doing about things. They had blown their guns just prior to 4 o'clock, and were moving to a rendezvous near Jarrer Park to camp with the other Batteries of their Regiment. There was enormous excitement and indignation as a gunner had just been killed by a shot from a sniper's rifle fired from one of the tenement houses in the neighbourhood. They had an idea from where the shot came and were determined that their comrade's death should be avenged. I did not wait to discover the outcome. The locality was obviously dangerous and I did not want to be a target for other snipers.

Bombing had continued all day and large numbers of planes were never absent from the sky. A vast pall of smoke and dust hung over Singapore. As one looked down Serangoon Road, one's eyes could not pierce the thick fog. The sun shone uncannily through the haze, creating an atmosphere of impending doom.

The casualties amongst civilians must have been enormous, as the Japs had assiduously bombed and shelled the heavily-built-on native quarters and the city proper. By 5.30 pm, civilians emerged from their retreats and some were openly walking up and down the road.

The Indian troops were in great fettle, laughing and joking. They had previously asked me if I could spare any beer or spirits, so I let them have all we had in the Mess wagon, with the exception of a bottle or two of whisky, some beer, and brandy that I thought might come in useful. Asking my permission was only a formality really, as the Sikhs had already looted the Mess stores pretty thoroughly and some of them were decidedly merry - but what was the use of interfering. My orderly, Ahmed Khan, rescued the liquor that I required, with some difficulty I gathered, so I decided to let the Sikhs have the rest.

At dusk, orders arrived to go to the Polo Ground, where the rest of the Regiment would foregather. I packed all my bedding and my belongings in my car. Whilst supervising the packing of the mess paraphernalia into HQ mess lorry - who should arrive but Ronald Coleman, D-B, Dizzy Coleman and three others.

Ronald and I withdrew out of earshot of the troops and he told me that they were going to have a shot at escape, would I join them? I agreed immediately. Within five minutes, having collected a spare shirt, some tins of bully, cigarettes, and matches, I was seated in Ronald's car and driving down Lavender Street en route to Kallang, which I had suggested as the nearest place that might be possible to secure a boat.

There was no moon and the night was as black as ink. We drove with headlights full on, for we never passed a person on our way to Kallang. The road was potholed with bomb and shell craters, and tram and electric cable wires were strewn over the roads. Crossing over the bridge near the Gas Works, we pulled up on the side of the road about 100 yards on the seaside of the bridge.

Whilst the others searched the river banks, I decided to find out if anyone was aboard any of the large craft anchored or moored in the river. Most were anchored some distance out in the stream, but I managed to board one which had a narrow gangplank connecting it to the shore. It was about 80 feet long. Although I searched, I could find no one aboard. However, tied up alongside was another Tongkang, onto which I scrambled.

I was challenged by a Chinese voice from its bowels. I replied that I was a British officer trying to escape as the Japanese were now in possession of Singapore. I explained that we wanted his assistance and that we were prepared to take any suitable junk. The person would not emerge and told me that he would not help. I offered him $500 (one of the officers had his battery funds on him) but he was not impressed. I then told him that in addition to the $500 cash we would give him $500 per head on arrival in Java or Sumatra, but even this would not move him.

All these negotiations had to be carried on in a whisper, because we knew that the aerodrome on the other side of the river was in the hands of the Japs. We also had to be on our guard against our own patrols whom we knew had orders to fire on anyone attempting to escape. Later, we heard that this had actually occurred.

I realised that it was useless to try and enlist the help of this individual, but I also realised that it would be stupid for us to attempt a get-away on our own. One could only get out of the Kallang river on a high tide, following a narrow channel through the mud. Apart from this, a junk is a most unwieldy vessel to sail unless one has experience of them, and none of us had.

The others had searched the river-bank for several hundred yards but no small craft were available at all. Nor could we find anyone who might help in sailing one of the large tongkangs. So, we decided to go to the Yacht Club and see if there were any facilities for getting away. We all bundled into the car again and set off along Beach Road and past Raffles. We had to drive with care, due to the usual debris - shell-holes, wires, overturned cars etc.

It was like a city of the dead. After crossing the Anderson bridge, the road was congested with hundreds of empty cars - all crowded together in wild confusion. This mass of cars extended from the bridge to the other side of Clifford Pier, overflowing down Battery Road. There was a lane through this multitude of cars just wide enough for a lorry to negotiate.

It was a pitiable sight to see these derelict cars - the majority of which were plainly the erstwhile pride of their owners. I could picture the crowds swarming to the pier on hearing the news of the impending capitulation - all in desperate hope of being able to escape. Vessels belonging to Customs, Police, Harbour Board, business houses etc were probably all impressed to get hundreds, maybe thousands, of civilians and military away from the doomed island. So I mused, as we drove along.

After leaving Clifford Pier we passed burning warehouses between us and the sea. Turning left to the Yacht Club, it seemed that all the buildings and warehouses in the neighbourhood were on fire. The place was a perfect inferno.

We had to leave the car 200 yards from the Yacht Club, as there were several bomb craters in the road and the place was cluttered with cars, lorries, and debris. From outside the Club, it was obvious that a large party was going on inside. We had neither the time nor the inclination to participate. Instead, we made our way to the slipway and boat sheds, where twenty or thirty others were engaged on the same task of trying to find a suitable craft. No Yacht Club employees could be found. I even went to their quarters. There were several yachts tied up to buoys in the basin, but it was obvious that sails and rudders would be kept in lockers in the club. It would be impossible in the dark to tell which sails belonged to which yacht. Unfortunately, a yacht seemed to be out of the question.

Lights were forbidden by general consent, and loud were the imprecations if someone unwittingly lit a cigarette. On one occasion, a rifle was fired from the P&O wharf, and a bullet whistled unpleasantly near. The night was pitch black and it was difficult to keep our party together. We found some prams (miniature broad-beamed yachts capable of carrying two persons) and after a lot of labour and sweat, succeeded in launching one. It half filled with water while trying to push it through the barbed-wire which fringed the shore. A few minutes later it almost filled with water and was very difficult to control in the choppy waves.

Our party was too large for the pram in any case. Someone had found a couple of oars, but even so, I was not particularly sorry when we agreed that the pram scheme was impractical. I did not want to give up until it was quite clear that escape was impossible, and Dizzy felt similarly. I thought that the two of us could manage a pram, but on our return all the prams had disappeared.

We went along the beach and, to my surprise, came to a large boat-shed and jetty - part of the Yacht Club which I had been unaware of. There were 50 people there and a fine large yacht moored alongside the jetty. However, they refused to take any more on board and sailed shortly after. In midstream, there was another 6 metre-type vessel preparing to sail.

In a boatshed nearby, there were numbers of whaleboats - vast, heavy craft. I helped push them into the water, but they were dry and the seams were open. It was probably years since they had last been in the water, and they filled up quickly. It was a pity, as one could have accommodated 20 or 30 people with ease.

I met Jim Davidson from Alor Star who told me that he had a launch anchored close to the shore - but no petrol. This could be easily remedied! I had met Stubbs in the throng only a few minutes before and it was the work of only a few seconds to find him again and explain the position. Jim Davidson promised him a passage if he could find 40 gallons of petrol.

I accompanied Jim in a tour of the basin in a small dug-out. When we were both seated we had 2 inches of freeboard. There was the never-absent expectation of being tipped into the water at any instant. He sat in the stern and paddled to where he said he had left the launch. Then he thought it might have been somewhere else. Finally, after paddling haphazardly all around the basin, he decided that someone had stolen it and we returned to the jetty. Shortly after,

Stubbs arrived with 70 gallons of petrol and I left Jim to explain why it was of no use.

By about 4 o'clock, I could hardly stand. Lack of sleep and the strain of the last few days was having its effect. My limbs felt like lead and I could only keep awake with difficulty. I did not know the time the Japanese would be entering Singapore. It could be daybreak and I had no desire to be captured by them whilst alone - in case they were in a spiteful mood. Added to this thought was the inadvisability of returning late to the Regiment - as I had no wish to be regarded a deserter.

In the circumstances, it seemed sensible to give up the idea of escape for the time being. I returned to the Yacht Club House, and met a Volunteer Officer named Longmore en route. He was of the same mind as myself. Sounds of carousal could still be heard in the Yacht Club. There were several cars parked outside. Ignition keys were missing from all of them but I eventually found a Marmon Harrington which started immediately. Longmore suggested I stay the night with the Volunteers in the Girls School Building alongside the Convent, as I might not find the Regiment easily. I slept on an unoccupied camp bed and slept like a log until about 6.30, when I was roused by the general bustle.

16th February

My truck was outside where I had left it. I had to drive carefully through the indescribable mess that the streets were in. I reached the Polo Ground in ten minutes, and to my relief found that the Regiment was there. The vehicles were drawn up in lines across the Polo Ground, with about 15 feet between each. The Indians were all busy cooking their food, washing their clothes etc. Many were stretched out under the vehicles or in the open, still sleeping.

I reported to the Colonel immediately on arrival - merely mentioning that that I had been prevented from joining the Regiment during the night. He knew, of course, the reason for my late arrival, but tactfully asked no questions and merely said that he was glad to see that I was fit and well.

I enquired where my car was parked and was told by the Doctor that shortly after I left RHQ the previous night, orders had been given to go to the Polo ground. He had detailed someone to bring my car around, but it could not be started and so the car was still near the Hindu Temple in Serangoon Road. The Marmon Harrington was still outside the Polo Ground so I hastily comandeered it once more, and drove around to the old camp site with my orderly. The car was not there, but numbers of articles that were formerly in the car were lying on the ground.

I went across to the small bungalow whose verandah we had used for messing, and found the owner, a Tamil doctor. He disclaimed any knowledge of the car but since I saw a tin box of mine which had been in the car on his kitchen verandah, I disbelieved him. Ahmad Khan found some other belongings of mine in the kitchen and also in the air-raid shelter.

I noticed that our activities were of great interest to some Tamils in one of the Temples. I decided to search the place, and sure enough found a few of my shirts and a pillow. Although I searched a few other buildings and ARP shelters in the vicinity, nothing more could be found, and I returned with my salvaged effects to the Polo Ground.

I had lost lots of useful clothing in addition to toilet requisites such as razors, toothbrush, brush and comb, mirror, etc. However, I decided my losses could I probably be made good as I had about $35. Apart from the possibility of buying the necessary articles, I knew that I could get a certain amount of clothing from Regimental reserve stores - with which at least one of our trucks was filled.

A good alfresco breakfast was served about 9 o'clock. Tinned fish, tinned sausages and tomatoes, fried potatoes, biscuits and coffee. Whilst we were having this breakfast, a large Jap bomber zoomed across the Polo Ground, barely 200 feet up. One's first reaction was an urgent desire to hear the patter of machine gun fire directed against the plane daring to fly so low. This was our first tangible reminder that we were all prisoners of the Japanese, and that all our future existence depended on our captor's goodwill.

None of discussed the possibility of future torture or shootings, but the possibility was not far from any of our minds. In addition to our own vehicles, there were also a large number of RASC vehicles. A number of RASC officers were billeted in the pavilion and RASC other ranks were living in tents. The stables were stacked to the roof with cases of tinned food and there were two large dumps of cases in the open in front of the pavilion.

At about 10 o'clock, the first enemy Japanese who I could recognise as such (for doubtless I had seen a number disguised as Chinese in Malaya) arrived at the Polo Ground on a motor bike. He was an 'other rank' as he had a rifle slung over his shoulder.

After a few minutes, he was followed by several other Japs who arrived in cars. This party included several officers.

On their arrival, I moved away from the Pavilion as the Japs might have disliked being stared at.

The party walked into the pavilion and appeared to engage in conversation with the RASC officers. A few minutes later a messenger brought over a request from the RASC Group asking for anyone who could speak Malay, to assist as an interpreter, The Colonel deputed me. There were three Jap officers seated in the pavilion, one of whom bade me in Malay to be seated. He then put a number of questions to the senior RASC officer, through me, as to the number of RASC personnel etc on the Polo Ground. Later on, Colonel Hughes was asked similar questions. All the information sought was of this character, and having discovered what they wanted, they demanded food. I told them lunch would be ready in about an hour, asking them if they would have lunch with us. They assented and expressed their thanks.

Only one of the Japanese spoke Malay (which he did with fluency) and although I tried tactfully to unearth his antecedents he did not satisfy my curiosity, except to inform me that he had been in KL whilst it was being attacked by the Japanese. He was a young man aged about 24, slim and good-looking. He was tall for a Jap, and would have passed for either a Chinese or Malay in appearance.

Whilst waiting for lunch, we were joined by another two Jap officers who were extremely polite and were introduced to us by name. They shook hands and seated themselves. However, after a discussion with their colleagues, they went off. Our guests divested themselves of their long swords and sword-belts and asked for hot water and the loan of shaving kit to rid themselves of several days growth of beard. It was obvious that they had not changed their clothes nor shaved for a considerable time. Continual and barely-concealed yawning, every now and then, bespoke lack of sleep.

When lunch was put on the table, the three Jap officers sat down with us and each put away a very respectable amount of food. It was clear that English food was much appreciated.

The Jap told us that no soldier was to leave the Polo Ground under any circumstances - for he would be liable to be shot on sight outside. He told us amongst other things that the Japanese were taking measures for the prevention of looting in the city. The penalty was death.

Quite a number of Japanese put in an appearance during the afternoon. They received their instructions and went off again. One of our guests was a major and seemed to be a person of some consequence.

Various orders from RA Brigade HQ and from RASC HQ kept arriving during the day. I had to interpret each one to the Japs before they would allow it to go to its destination. All this happened in a civilised way - which heartened us all. There is no doubt that we had expected to be treated quite differently.

At about 4 o'clock, the Jap Major had apparently received his orders from his superior authority concerning our arms. These had been dealt with shortly after the Japs' arrival in the morning - rifles in one heap - revolvers in another heap - bren and automatic guns in another - SA ammunition - hand grenades - tommy guns - binoculars etc - all in separate heaps.

He ordered us to provide lorries to transport the arms and ammunition to some unknown destination, also drivers and a certain number of men to load the lorries. These orders were quickly carried out. By dark, all arms and ammunition had been taken away.

After a bath, officers congregated in and around our Mess tent - some on camp stools, others on the ground. Orderlies dispensed drinks (of which we possessed ample). By the time dinner was ready, everyone was in a most convivial mood. On this occasion, the Colonel decreed that our signal section NCO's could join us at dinner. This was a thoughtful act which gratified everyone. They had done excellent work during the campaign and it would have been churlish if we European officers had not included our three British 'other ranks'.

Toasts were drunk during and after dinner, and speeches were made. It was a pathetic event in a way - made more so by the superficial gaiety with which we were all endowed. Everyone was slightly drunk.

The Doctor and Lt Pershotan Das were the only two Indian Officers present, being King's commissioned officers. The VCO's had a party of their own. The hilarity increased as the evening wore on until our stock of liquor was finished. God Save The King was sung - and so to bed.

17th February

It was a fine sunny morning. Our appreciation of it was spoilt by the foetid odours of decaying corpses which were lying in a sort of infirmary next door to the Police Station. We had not attempted to do anything about their disposal as we hoped friends or relatives would attend to it. However, the smell was now so bad that several of the officers went in to investigate. They found a large number of decrepit and diseased Asiatics of both sexes who appeared to be half-starved wandering around. In an out-house they found about twenty corpses which they burnt.

During the morning, it was ordered that all books and papers should be destroyed. Fortunately, this was obeyed only to a limited extent. Orders were also received that all British Prisoners Of War would be accommodated in Changi Barracks. There were details of times of leaving, orders of march etc. Indian POW were to proceed to Farrer Park, and similar details were supplied for their direction.

We were told we could take one lorry to transport kit and food. Everyone would proceed on foot apart from the lorry driver and one other. Again the orders were disregarded and the remainder of the morning was spent loading up two of the largest lorries with cases of beef, milk, sugar, and every other article which that might be useful. We were advised to bring tents, oil stoves, kerosene, petrol, digging implements etc. A large amount of personal kit had to be discarded in order to provide space for essential articles and food. As a result, I was able to collect sufficient clothing here and there to bring my kit up to strength.

In the Polo Pavilion, I found several tubes of toothpaste, shaving gear etc. I dispensed these to other officers, reserving sufficient for myself. In the Club stables, I found cases of Gold Flake cigarettes in cartons and secured 6,000 cigarettes. None of the other officers took advantage of this windfall - an omission they regretted later. So the morning passed, and at 1 o'clock the Indians were paraded, each carrying what personal belongings he could.

THE END

Appendix 1

The Road to Singapore
From Alor Star to Singapore

THE MALAYAN PENINSULA

Appendix 2
Eden Hall

Eden Hall is currently the British High Commissioner's residence in Singapore. It was built in 1904 for Ezekiel Saleh Manasseh, on a four and a half-acre plot, which used to be part of a nutmeg plantation. A wide verandah runs round the house, both upstairs and down.

In 1916 Ezekiel Manasseh married an English widow, Elsie Trilby Bath, whose husband had been a mining engineer in Pahang. They moved to Eden Hall with Trilby's two children Molly and Vivian.

Molly later married a renowned surgeon, Arthur Dickson Wright, of St Mary's Hospital, London and one of their daughters was Clarissa Dickson Wright, the acclaimed chef (one of the "Two Fat Ladies").

Vivian attended school in Australia and England and returned to Singapore to join Lewis and Peat, a firm of rubber brokers. In common with the other well-heeled expatriates of the time, his social life revolved around horses and house parties.

At the outbreak of the Second World War, Vivian Bath joined the Singapore Volunteer Forces. With the surrender of the island he was captured and shipped to Hokkaido, where he was made to mine coal for the duration of the war.

Meanwhile, Eden Hall was commandeered by the Japanese Occupation Forces who used it as an officers' mess. By all accounts they took good care of the house and furniture, and left intact the wrought-iron staircase which has the initial

"M" incorporated into its design. Happily Manasseh had decided in the '30's to give the staircase a modern look by boarding up the ironwork and the Japanese never thought to look behind the boards.

On his return to Singapore after the war, Vivian Bath regained possession of Eden Hall, which had been requisitioned for use by the British forces. When Vivian Bath decided to retire to Australia, he sold Eden Hall to the British Government in 1957 for a nominal sum, with the stipulation that a plaque be installed at the bottom of the flagpole, which reads "May the Union Jack fly here forever".

In his memoirs, Lee Kuan Yew denotes a chapter to the famous "Eden Hall Tea Party", on 18 July 1961, a key meeting in the run-up to independence.

The Foreign and Commonwealth Office says it has worked hard to maintain the house in its original form. Although a new roof and bathrooms have been installed, the structure and fabric remain unchanged. Ezekiel Manasseh would have no difficulty in recognising his Edwardian "minor masterpiece".

Appendix 3
Just before Singapore fell (9.2.42)

-ORDER OF THE DAY

It is certain that pur troops on Singapore Island heavily outnumber any Japanese who have crossed the Straits. We must destroy them.
Our whole fighting reputation is at stake and the honour of the British Empire. The Americans have held out in the Bataan Peninsular against far heavier odds; the Russians are turning back the picked strength of the Germans; the Chinese with an almost complete lack of modern equipment have held the Japanese for four and a half years. It will be disgraceful if we yield our boasted fortress of Singapore to inferior enemy forces.
There must be no thought of sparing the troops or civilian population and no mercy must be shown to weakness in any shape or form. Commanders and Senior Officers must lead their men and if necessary die with them. There must be no question or thought of surrender. Every unit must fight it out to the end and in close contact with the enemy.
I look to you and to your men to fight to the end to prove that the fighting spirit that won our Empire still exists to enable us to defend it.

(sgd) A.P.WAVELL.

I attach a copy of an order I have received from the C in C

The gist of the order will be conveyed to all ranks through the medium of Commading Officers .

In some units the men have not shewn the fighting spirit which is to be expected of men of the British Empire.
It will be a lasting disgrace if we are def ated by an army of clever gangsters many times inferior in numbers to our men
The spirit of agression and determination to stick it out must be inculcated in all ranks. There must be no thought of further withdrawal without orders.
There are many fighting men moving about in the back areas. Every available man who is not doing essential work must be used to stop the invader.

Sgd. A.E. Percival Lt Gen
GOC Malaya

9-2-42

Appendix 4

After Singapore fell

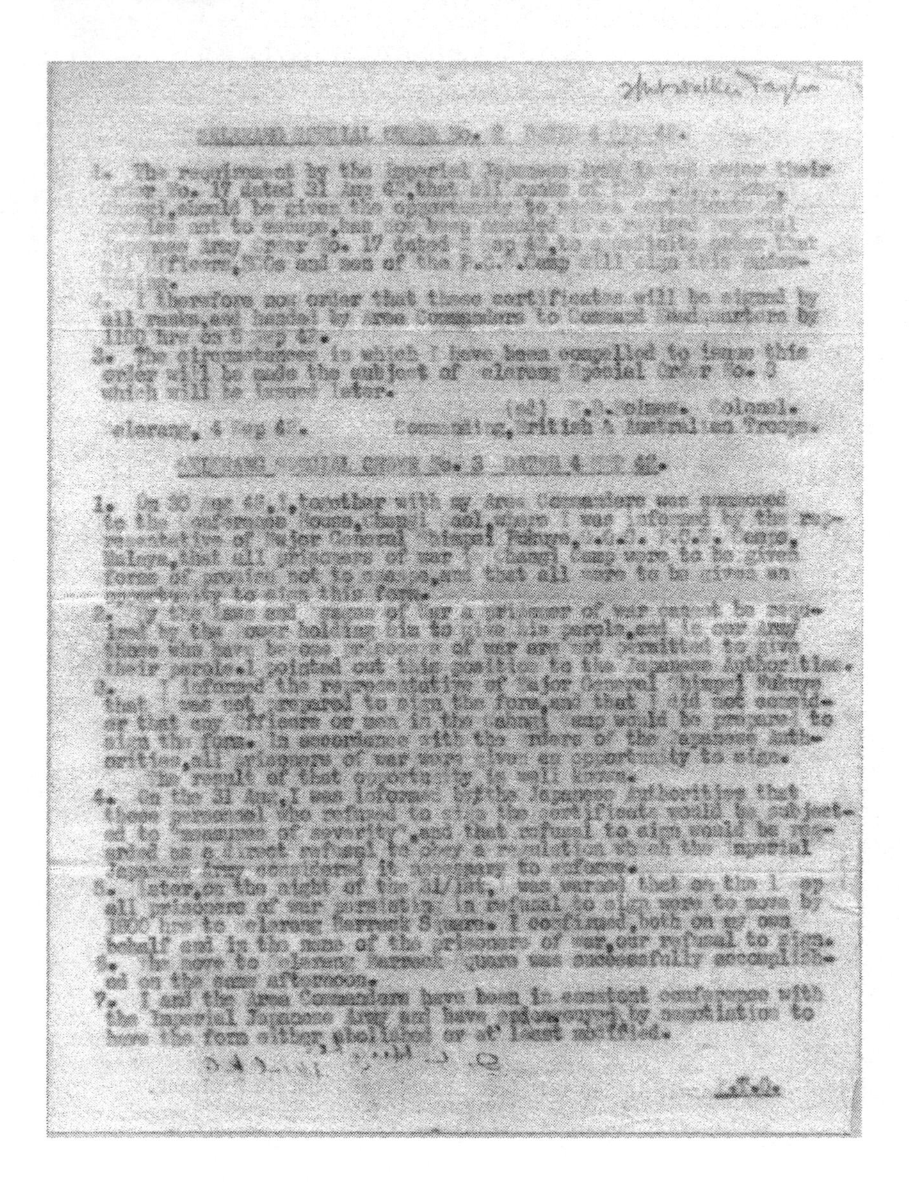

SELARANG SPECIAL ORDER No. 2 DATED 4 Sep 42.

1. The requirement by the Imperial Japanese Army [illegible] their Order No. 17 dated 31 Aug 42, that all ranks of the [illegible] Camp, Changi, should be given the opportunity to sign a certificate of promise not to escape, has now been amended in a revised Imperial Japanese Army Order No. 17 dated 2 Sep 42, to a definite order that all Officers, NCOs and men of the P.O.W. Camp will sign this undertaking.
2. I therefore now order that these certificates will be signed by all ranks, and handed by Area Commanders to Command Headquarters by 1100 hrs on 5 Sep 42.
3. The circumstances in which I have been compelled to issue this order will be made the subject of Selarang Special Order No. 3 which will be issued later.

(sd) E.B. Holmes. Colonel.

Selarang, 4 Sep 42. Commanding, British & Australian Troops.

SELARANG SPECIAL ORDER No. 3 DATED 4 Sep 42.

1. On 30 Aug 42, I, together with my Area Commanders was summoned to the Conference House, Changi Gaol, where I was informed by the representative of Major General Shimpei Fukuye, G.O.C. P.O.W. Camps, Malaya, that all prisoners of war in Changi Camp were to be given forms of promise not to escape, and that all were to be given an opportunity to sign this form.
2. By the laws and usages of war a prisoner of war cannot be required by the power holding him to give his parole, and in our Army those who have become prisoners of war are not permitted to give their parole. I pointed out this position to the Japanese Authorities.
3. I informed the representative of Major General Shimpei Fukuye that I was not prepared to sign the form, and that I did not consider that any Officers or men in the Changi Camp would be prepared to sign the form. In accordance with the orders of the Japanese Authorities, all prisoners of war were given an opportunity to sign.
The result of that opportunity is well known.
4. On the 31 Aug, I was informed by the Japanese Authorities that those personnel who refused to sign the certificate would be subjected to "measures of severity", and that refusal to sign would be regarded as a direct refusal to obey a regulation which the Imperial Japanese Army considered it necessary to enforce.
5. Later, on the night of the 31/1st, I was warned that on the 1 Sep all prisoners of war persisting in refusal to sign were to move by 1800 hrs to Selarang Barrack Square. I confirmed, both on my own behalf and in the name of the prisoners of war, our refusal to sign.
6. The move to Selarang Barrack Square was successfully accomplished on the same afternoon.
7. I and the Area Commanders have been in constant conference with the Imperial Japanese Army and have endeavoured, by negotiation to have the form either abolished or at least modified.

Appendix 4 (ctd)

After Singapore fell (16.9.42)

All that I have been able to obtain is that that which was originally a demand, accompanied by threats of "measures of severity", has now been issued as an official order of the Imperial Japanese Government.

8. During the period of the occupation of the Selarang Barrack Square the conditions in which we have been placed have been under my constant consideration. These may briefly be described as such that existence therein will result in a very few days in the outbreak of epidemic and the most serious consequences to those under my command and inevitable death to many. Taking into account the low state of health in which many of us now are, and the need to preserve our force intact as long as possible, and in the full conviction that my action, were the circumstances in which we are now living known to them, would meet with the approval of His Majesty's Government, I have felt it my duty to order all personnel to sign the certificate under the duress imposed by the Imperial Japanese Army.

9. I am fully convinced that His Majesty's Government only expects prisoners of war not to give their parole when such parole is to be given voluntarily. This factor can in no circumstances be regarded as applicable to our present condition. The responsibility for this decision rests with me, and with me alone, and I fully accept it in ordering you to sign.

10. I wish to record in this Order my deep appreciation of the excellent spirit and good discipline which all ranks have shown during this trying period. I look to all ranks to continue in good heart, discipline and morale. Thank you all for your loyalty and co-operation.

(sd) E.B.Holmes. Colonel.

Selarang. 4 Sep 42. Commanding, British & Australian Troops.

COPY OF LETTER No. SELERANG A1/A DATED 4 SEP 42.

Reference Selarang Special Order No. 3 dated 4 Sep 42.

My attention has been drawn to some concern which is being felt that there may be adverse financial consequences on individuals as the result of the signing of the non-escape certificate.

It is obviously impossible for me to give a ruling in this matter which must rest in other hands than mine. I wish, however, all ranks to be informed that this point had my full consideration at the time of the decision, and I am convinced that no such adverse consequence to pay, pension or allowances will result to any individual. It will naturally be my first endeavour, also, to ensure on release that the position is made clear to His Majesty's Government.

(sd) E.B.Holmes. Colonel.

Changi, 4 Sep 42. Commanding, British & Australian Troops.

Certified true copy.

G. L. Hughes Lt/Col RA

Changi, 16 Sep 42. Commanding, 22nd Mountain Regiment.

Appendix 5
First notification to Pat of Basil's survival

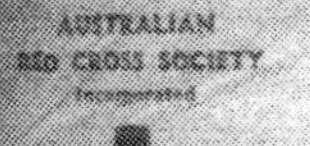

AUSTRALIAN
RED CROSS SOCIETY

S.A. DIVISION

RED CROSS BUREAU FOR
WOUNDED, MISSING & PRISONERS OF WAR

1st FLOOR, RED CROSS HOUSE
61-63 GAWLER PLACE
ADELAIDE

FC
B.7616.

PHONE: C. 8420

5th February, 1943.

Mrs. B.P. Walker-Taylor,
17 Thornber Street,
UNLEY PARK.

Dear Madam,

Re 2nd Lieut. Basil Patteson, WALKER-TAYLOR.

As the result of enquiries on your behalf for the abovenamed, we wish to advise that a cable has been received from Tokio through the International Red Cross Society stating that 2nd Lieut. B.P. Walker-Taylor of the 11th Division is a Prisoner of War in Malaya Camp.

We are very glad to be able to pass on this reassuring news to you. Enclosed please find the latest pamphlet giving instructions concerning letters to Prisoners in Japanese controlled areas.

Yours faithfully,

Annie E. Simonett

Mrs. A.E. Simonett,
DIRECTOR.

Appendix 6

Picture drawn of Basil Walker-Taylor in Changi Gaol By a fellow prisoner 21.6.45

Appendix 7

Basil and Pat Walker-Taylor
Martin Place, Sydney, Oct 1945

Appendix 8

People mentioned in the diary

FAMILY

Surname	First name	Relationship
Walker-Taylor	Basil	Author
Walker-Taylor	Pat	Basil's wife
Walker-Taylor	Lois	Basil's sister
Barr	Millie (Mum)	Pat's mother
Hall	Elsie	Pat's sister
Hall	Bill	her husband
Barr	Derek	Pat's brother
Barr	Olive	his wife
Barr	Cedric	his son
Barr	Robert	his son
Mannasseh	Aunty Trilby	Millie's sister
Mannasseh	Uncle Eze	Trilby's second husband
Gordon	Uncle Dick	Millie's brother
Gordon	Aunty May	his wife
Bath	Vivian	Trilby's son (first marriage)

NON-FAMILY

Surname	First name	Rank	Page Refs
Ah Qwee			24
Ah Seow			14,15,24
Alsagoff			108
Armstrong			11,14,16
Bancroft			15,17,17,20,21,22,24,25,27,28
Beattie	David		27
Biddulph			15,17,18
Black	Drummond	Lt	59
Blackman			18
Boissier			17
Bridges			85
Cameron		Sgt Major	33